JOURNEY
FOR THE
KING

THE
FAITH
WALKER

BOBBY DENDY

аBM

NEVER
GIVE UP!

Published by:
A Book's Mind
PO Box 272847
Fort Collins, CO 80527

Copyright © 2020
ISBN: 978-1-949563-80-1
Printed in the United States of America

FOREWORD
PART 1

My cell phone rang and when I answered it, I was surprised to hear the voice of one of our friends. John Lenard, in Kerrville, Texas on the line. My husband Lyle and I were at our vacation home in Port Lavaca relaxing and doing a little fishing. John Lenard explained to me that there was a man, by the name of Bobby Dendy, visiting The Coming King Foundation (TCKF), prayer garden in Kerrville. At that time, there was nothing on the mountain except a giant 77-foot core tin metal cross surrounded by dirt and rocks. Bobby, along with 3 of his friends from Phoenix, were there playing worship music and enjoying the presence of God on the mountain.

Bobby had seen the Cross on the mountain as he was traveling to South Carolina a few days prior and upon seeing that the grand opening was just a few days away, felt led of the Lord to stay. When Bobby arrived, he said he felt the presence of God so strongly and knew he had to call his friends from Phoenix to come and experience the awesome presence of God on the mountain. John was on the board of TCKF and asked us if they could stay in my guest house and I gladly said,

"Of course! The house is open, tell them to make themselves at home and I will be home in a few days."

When we returned home, I found Bobby and his friends doing well in my guest house. What was intended to be a 7-day commitment that was agreed upon by the President of the foundation, Max Greiner, turned into a 40-day adventure where Bobby installed rock speakers and an iPod that played worship music 24 hours a day at the Cross. The music that was installed by Bobby in 2012 is still playing to this day.

Many people were touched and transformed by encountering the presence of God while Bobby was there on the mountain. Many accepted Christ as their Savior and were healed of various sicknesses and maladies. This was my first encounter with DJ Bobby Dendy.

We have stayed in touch through the years and we talk almost daily. Bobby continues to travel wherever the Lord leads him to play worship music and create a space for the presence of God to encounter the lives of the people there. He totally lives by faith and it is amazing to see how the Lord has and continues to provide for him. Bobby is an incredibly talented artist, working in several different mediums. But listening to his story of God asking him to give everything up to follow Jesus is remarkable and shows in his Faith today.

He has been used, abused, and blessed by the Christian community but God has never failed him. Many do not understand his mission to follow the Lord and go where he is sent but this is Bobby's journey and his faith won't allow him not to obey. Even if that has meant at times being asked to come and play worship music and never receiving any financial aid. On one occasion he was invited to come to Texas and play for several days. That is a 20 hour drive one way. It rained almost the whole time and he spent his nights in a small entrance building on the grounds playing worship music and ministering to hurting people. When his commitment was over, no honorarium was offered and he left to go back to Arizona, with a half tank of gas and $40.00 in his pocket. He called me when his truck was on empty and he was sitting at a truck stop somewhere in Texas. He told me about the amazing things that happened and how God is always faithful. I felt compelled to wire him money to get him back to Phoenix.

On another occasion, he was playing worship music for a large conference in Arizona. He stayed outside in a tent where it rained almost the whole week and when it was over, no honorarium was offered, everyone left, and Bobby was left with his truck stuck in the mud. If you ask Bobby about incidents like these, he will only answer, "It's all about Jesus and being obedient to go where he asks me to go." That's faith! There are so many stories to tell and Bobby does it very well in this book. He has almost daily encounters with individuals on the street and in various places where he tells them about Jesus and many times gives them his last penny at the leading of the Holy Spirit.

Ever since I have met Bobby, I have been aware of God's anointing on his life and the presence of God that abides there. As time has gone on, I have seen the anointing increase exponentially as he continues to follow the leading of the Holy Spirit. If you ask Bobby about his life and where God is taking him, he will only reply, "Just Jesus."

Patsy J. Jordan

FOREWORD
PART 2

If you are reading this right now, this is not happenstance. This book is on your radar because God has an amazing message for you via the life of his servant DJ Bobby Dendy. Without question, you will be blessed and enlightened by the reading of this book.

Phenomenal obedience and resilience are major themes in this narrative. When it comes to walking with the Lord, Bobby Dendy is the very definition and personification of these concepts.

I have blessed so many people with Bobby Dendy's anointed Christian music compilations and have listened to them every night for years. I am commonly told the music fills the place it is played with peace.

Folks in my life know about the day God sent a new client and perfect stranger to my job and she passed on Dendy's musical message to me and directed me to a church. I smiled, thanked her for the information but let it pass in one ear and out of the other. Later, a move of God on my heart had me drive directly to that church after work that same day.

I walked into Cathedral Christian Center in Phoenix, which most definitely housed an active and palatable presence of God at around 6 pm and left at midnight. When I stepped into the church, the atmosphere was alive with warmth and wonder, there were people scattered about in the pews and at the alter praying. I sat down and basked in this deep transformative feeling known as God's anointing. Though Dendy and other people offered to pray with and for me, I wanted no contact. I was confused as to why I was there and was not in a social mood. I continued to spend every available moment at the church with this fantastic music, being spoken to by God, ministered to by the Holy Spirit and eventually prayed for by Dendy. In that church, I encountered open heavens, angelic visitations, and a miraculous cleansing of my spirit. I was in awe, and was not quite sure of what was happening, but I could not get enough of it.

That was more than a decade ago, since our first meeting I have watched God use Dendy's servant's heart to connect, bless, inspire, guide, encourage, pray for, champion, and redirect many brothers and sisters in their walk with Christ. God even sent Bobby Dendy to literally save my life!

My dear friend Bobby is an American missionary, whom I have witnessed the Lord use fearlessly and lovingly to minister to the whole societal spectrum from homeless drug addicts, gun toting pimps, and lost prostitutes to burnt out professionals and multi-millionaires. As well, I have watched the Lord reward Bobby for his faithful obedience. I have met many individuals with broken spirits, who are desperately seeking healing, or a change in their own lives. When they meet Bobby they can feel the power of the energy field that he carries and they ask what is that? And Dendy answers, "Just Jesus!"

You have probably never heard a story like this one, it's main character a general in the Army of God, winning souls for the Kingdom of God through music, sacrifice and selfless giving. It is mission that few would accept or survive without knowing who you are in Christ.

In many ways this story is unbelievable, but I know it is true. Read on and be blessed and encouraged.

By Dr. Jamise Grace Liddell

CONTENTS

PART I

INTRODUCTION

~

If it were easy being a Christian, why are there not more? That thought has always been in the forefront of my mind. Being a follower of Christ has never been boring. I thought before I came to Christ that Christians were boring and why in the world would I want to become one? You see, I was a nightclub entertainer and Disc Jockey for fourteen years. Life was full of excitement and drama every night with the pounding of the music, the flashing lights and everything else that went with being the center of the club scene. The idea of going to church on Sundays was out of the picture for me, even though I had been invited many times. However, I'm so thankful that I had a praying mother that never gave up on the promises she had from the Lord about my life. I'm so grateful that my mother prayed for me all those years to come to Christ and serve Him. I gave my life over to JESUS CHRIST in January of 1990. The stories in this journey are just some of hundreds that have happened over the past eighteen years that I have been a Christian. The pages are filled with tears, laughter, healing and the miracles after miracles that have taken place and are still taking place in my life and my family's lives as I write this story today. I hope and pray that you will find something in the pages of this book that will encourage, challenge and prompt you to follow Christ.

1

THERE WILL BE PLENTY OF TIME TO CRY

~

It was July 7, 2006 and my wife had had enough. She looked at me and said, "I want you to leave this house and I want you to leave right now." I just stood there in a daze and thought, "She can't be serious. She'll give me one more chance. She always gives me one more chance." This time, however, it was different. There was a serious resolve to her voice that I had never heard before. I just stood there as a flood of pain rushed through my heart and then made its way up to my head. My wife looked at me and said, "I'm done with this ministry being a way to support our family. I want you to get a full-time job, a real job, and do ministry in your spare time." As I heard the words come out of her mouth, I thought, "Spare time? What spare time?" We have a full-time epidemic of broken and hurting youth in this country with more than fifty percent of the youth coming from broken and fatherless homes. I thought, "When, and how, do I give the youth my 'spare time' when my own children need more time with me?" My thoughts were rushing like a flashflood down a dry riverbed. I started calculating in my head the weekly time needed for my family. Meanwhile, my wife stood there looking at me, waiting for a reply.

This is how it was playing out in my head: forty hours a week at a full-time job, my three girls (Kristyn 16, Keeley 10, & Casidie 8 and autistic) need time with me each day after school and before bed, and my wife needed her time as well. She worked a full-time job and was out of the house ten hours a day, five days a week. Right now I was home every day to take care of the girls and get them off to school, then

3

do the laundry, wash the dishes and clean the house. I also worked as a Corporate DJ and entertainer one or two nights a week during the peak season in Phoenix. The pay was good. I would make in one night what most people made in a week. The challenge was that the season was only from October through May in Phoenix, and the summer was very slow. All of the requests I would get for ministry events would be for the weekends and none of these events even came close to paying me what I would get as a Corporate DJ. Most times, I would not break even and this would drive my wife crazy. The Lord would show up at these events and lives would be touched and changed, but we were the ones who would suffer financially for not taking the Corporate DJ events instead.

It wasn't that we didn't have a burden for the youth; it was that we couldn't get any financial help so that we could minister to the youth and still survive. It has always amazed me how we, as the church, can help people around the world but we can't help our own youth in this country.

While all of this was going on in my head, my wife was still looking at me and waiting for an answer. I was waiting for the Lord to download an answer, and fast. If I worked a full-time day job, I wouldn't have any time left for the full-time call that was on my life and my family together. I couldn't just run off on the weekends and not have them with me. We've had this discussion more than once over the twelve years of our marriage and my wife has sacrificed, and believes 1,000 times more than any woman I could possibly imagine. Yet, I was asking her to hang on just a little bit longer. One more day. We were almost at the breakthrough point to be funded to do this as a family and become missionaries to our own country.

The Lord did not download a response to my wife's request and she looked at me in pain and disbelief and said, "You need to get your things and leave now!" In those twelve years of marriage I had never been away from my family for more than a day or two. As the reality of my situation started to sink in, I just went numb. I kept thinking, "Lord, where are you?" Then I heard these words from the Lord, "There will be plenty of time to cry, get your things and do as your wife asked." So, I gathered some clothes, a sleeping bag, and a pillow and told my children that Dad was going to be gone for a little while, but I would be back soon. I put everything in the van, told my wife that I loved her and left.

I wish I could tell you that things got better right away and that God fixed it the next day, but that is not the truth. I was about to go on a journey through pain and tears that would forever change my life and many others' along the way.

2

LOVE HER AND LET GOD DO THE REST

~

Our life with Christ is a journey. It is an amazing ride if you choose to get on board and strap yourself in. Disneyland is nothing in comparison. The Lord never promised it would be easy, He only promised that He would never leave us or forsake us. I needed to trust in this now more than ever.

Before I left my home that night, I told my wife that I would be back in a day or two to pick up the rest of my clothes and all of my DJ equipment. I really didn't have a clue as to where or what I was going to do, so I drove about 60 miles west of Phoenix to see a couple of friends who owned an old west RV park. As I drove down the two-lane road, I just started to cry and call out to the Lord.

Before the Lord brought us together, my wife had been divorced for a short time after her first marriage of five years had come to an end. When we got married in 1994, my stepdaughter Kristyn was four years old. Within a couple of years, our two other daughters, Keeley and Casidie were born. God has blessed me with such a beautiful family. My wife and I had been through so much together over the past twelve years. We had been united in our common vision for youth ministry from the time the Lord brought us together. She also has a burden for the youth of this country and when we first got married, we both saw the need for a Christian Youth Club for teens.

Also, early on in our marriage, I was producing a radio show called "Radio Hope" in Phoenix at a small station called KRDS. Over the 3 years I worked there, God blessed the show beyond our expectations, exploding the program across 10 cities nationwide. Our dreams and desires to reach the youth were alive and full of hope. However, during our years of marriage and ministry, we endured a lot of pain and disappointment from various churches and other ministries. It has always amazed me how within the church body we have done so much damage to our brothers and sisters in Christ. And now this unfortunate reality had started to take its toll on my own family.

As I drove on, thoughts and memories raced through my head. I realized that I had made many mistakes over the years and finding a balance in my life, my family and my ministry was going to be the key for the healing that we needed as a family. As I was reflecting on all we had gone through, the thought of my not being with my wife and my three girls was overwhelming. As I watched the big-rig trucks whiz by me on the opposite side of the road, I thought, "Maybe I was wrong all of these years to have put my wife and children through this." We had been a part of some amazing things and had been used by the Lord in ways that brought healing and deliverance to so many young people. It was never a question of whether or not the Lord was working through my family and me. It was a question of how could we do this and survive. The need was full-time and the support was little to nothing.

I thought, "My skills in the DJ secular arena are in high demand, and if I just worked at a steady job and went to church on Sunday like everyone else, we would be just fine." But I knew that the fire burning in me for the youth, and the need to take this to another level, would never ease up.

My mind continued to race over the events of the past few years and then a thought came to me. Maybe my family was better off without me. Just maybe their lives would have been easier if I wasn't around at all. The bright lights of the passing trucks seemed almost inviting. If I just pulled across the lane, the pain of all this would be over in a second. But that wasn't God's voice; it was the accuser's voice. As my hands gripped the steering wheel, I heard another voice, soothing and gentle say, "Just keep going, there will be plenty of time to cry. I AM with you."

The Lord began to comfort me and to remind me of the calling on my life and all the times He had orchestrated my life to bring me to the right place at the right time. I began to recall one divine encounter in particular, when I had met my friends Dorie and Jeff and first discovered my gift for Spirit-led worship.

For the past two years, I had been a part of a church of about sixty people called "The Source Worship Center" in Phoenix, Arizona. The pastors of the church were Dorie and Jeff Anderson. They had come from a crushing and painful experience at the hands of the leaders of their former church. A while back, one of my friends, Darryl Cottier, asked if I would visit Dorie and Jeff. He gave me their phone number and told me they were having a bible study in their home for their children and grandchildren. Darryl told me that Dorie and Jeff were instrumental in his ministry to reach the Rave Culture for Christ through Darryl's music outreach called, "DJ Darryl Urban Ministry of Sounds." Now Darryl is considered to be one of the best DJs and producers of dance music in the world. Anyway, at that time, I called and scheduled an appointment to speak with Jeff and Dorie at their home. When I arrived I shared with them some of the hurt, betrayal and disappointment with ministry that my family and I had been through. I was starting to tell Dorie about what I felt my family's calling to the Lord's plan was when she looked me in the eye and said, "Bobby, you don't need to share with me what God's plan is for you. He has already told me. When you walked through my door, I knew who you were."

As she continued to share with me the insights God had given to her about my life, I realized God had already spoken to Dorie about who I was and had led me to her and her family for a reason. I knew God was leading me to the right people, not only for my own encouragement, but for me to in turn encourage them.

A few days later I brought my DJ gear over to their house and set it up in their living room and played worship music as the Lord led me. That night, the Lord visited their home and began to bring healing to their family. For the past thirteen years, as I have played music unto the Lord, the Holy Spirit has always been faithful to show up and do some incredible things as the name of Jesus is lifted up. I will share just a few of those stories later on in the pages of this book. As always, the

Glory and Honor go to the Lord Jesus Christ and the working of the Holy Spirit. I have been called to bring heaven to Earth through worship. At that time, I couldn't see where this would lead, but now, looking back, I can see that it was only the beginning. Bringing this to the public and in a church setting.

Soon after I began doing worship in their home, they started hosting meetings centered on worship and teaching the Word. Then after a few meetings in their home, they were led to start a small church and I went with them to play worship music. We started out in a hotel, and eventually moved into a small shopping center in a part of Phoenix known for crystal meth, prostitution and violent crime. Pastor Dorie and Jeff are incredible people who love the Lord. They knew of the pain, disappointment and betrayal that had been brought on my family and me. They loved, supported and lifted my family and me up and believed in the call of the Lord on us to be missionaries to this country and this generation. They never forced me to bring my wife and children to church. After years of hanging on despite continuous experiences of hurt and betrayal, the heartache had finally become too much for my wife. Pastor Dorie and Jeff understood her pain. They told me to just love her and let God do the rest. My wife never stopped loving or believing in the Lord. She just wasn't willing to fall in love with God's people again, only to have them hurt her one more time. It hurt me so deeply to see my wife like this. However, through Pastor Dorie, Pastor Jeff and the other members of the Source Worship Center in Phoenix, I was recharged and equipped to go on. Through financial and prayerful support, they encouraged me and gave me faith to continue on with the calling that God had placed on our family. Most importantly of all, they believed in us, and, to this day, still do.

On my journeys over the past eighteen years, I can't tell you how many people I have come across with a similar story of pain who have told me that they never want anything to do with the church and God's people again. But we can't let our experience with people come before our calling and our relationship with God. People may betray you, but I've had an EXPERIENCE with the LOVE of God. It is this experience that becomes our strength. We should never believe that God doesn't love us. It is obvious that through His Son, Jesus Christ, He does and will forever be there for us.

3

LEANING ON THE ROCK

~

As I approached my friends' RV Park and pulled into the driveway of their restaurant there, I thought, "What should I tell my friends Kim and Jim?" They had been my friends for many years and I had met them through my wife, Cheryl. As I talked to both of them, they assured me everything would be okay. They asked if I would like to stay at the RV Park. They had plenty of room and they offered to let me stay as long as I liked. However, I felt in my heart that God was pushing me forward and that I had to follow. I wanted to stay, wanted to be comfortable, but God kept pushing me forward, pushing me into the unknown, and I just had to be obedient. So I thanked them and told the two of them I would talk to them later.

Kim and Jim had been in the stone and boulder business for many years and had just bought the RV Park a year earlier. I am a designer/artist in stone as well and have been working in stone for over twenty-five years. Once, we had talked about doing some projects with a stone that was very unusual and native to Arizona. It came from a particular quarry that Kim and Jim represented and they had already given me some of the stone to work with. I had created a few things in this stone that had gotten the attention of the owner of a stone company. Although I had been playing with this idea as a source of extra income for the past couple years, pursuing my design gift now seemed like a great possibility for moving things forward. My friends were sure something would come of this and it would be the answer to the financial challenge my family was facing. I had already visited the quarry of this northern Arizona stone company and had an open invitation to come back and stay for a while. They had even asked if I would be interested in moving to their small city to live and work there. At least I had something that I could pursue that looked promising; that could help get my family back on track.

As I drove back to Phoenix, I didn't have any idea where I was going to sleep that night. I decided to stop at a church just off the freeway. As I pulled into the church parking lot, I thought to myself, "What am I doing here?" I could have stayed at the RV Park. They had an extra bed and RV for me to use. My van was full of clothes, so I tilted my driver's side seat back and attempted to get some sleep. It was July in Phoenix and, even at midnight, it was still one hundred degrees. I think I closed my eyes for an hour or two and then went to McDonald's for coffee and breakfast at about 6:00 A.M. In McDonald's I was praying and asking God, "What in the world do I do now?" I pulled some papers out of my duffel bag and spotted the pages of what the Lord had had me working on for the past few months. I took all the pages out and spread them on the table in front of me. A few months earlier I had received a Christian magazine from my sister-in-law. In the magazine, they listed all the places, times and Christian artists performing at the Christian Music Festivals all over the United States during the upcoming summer months. I remember one time I was sitting at my kitchen table with the magazine and a U.S. atlas planning a route from Phoenix to every event I could get to across the country. I had calculated how many miles we would travel each day by RV, how much time we could spend in each city, and what we needed to get to and from each event across America. I calculated how much gas was going to cost for this trip and made note of what artist was at each event and so on. It took me about a month to plan this out. I couldn't stop myself. I knew it didn't make sense, but I told my wife I had to finish the plan. After I was done with the plan, my family and I would then attend over thirteen music festivals, driving through thirty states and 103 cities as we crisscrossed the U.S.

As I was looking at all these pages of the magazine in front of me, and eating my egg sandwich, I was recalling my wife asking me night after night as I sat at the kitchen table, "What are you doing this for? There is no way we can do this." I told her, "I'm not sure why the Lord has me doing this, but I can't stop until I'm done." Just then, the morning breakfast rush was coming into McDonalds's. People were walking by looking over my shoulder trying to figure what I was doing. I gathered up all the pages of this journey and put them back into my duffel bag.

Later that morning, I called Pastor Dorie and Jeff and told them about finding the papers again and feeling that God was going to do something with this. I also asked them if I could borrow the RV that their church owned. It was an older RV I had used many times for outreach events. I told them that I didn't think I would need to use it for very long. I just needed a place to live for now. They agreed to let me use it as long as I needed. I went back home to pick up my 6x10 foot enclosed trailer with all my DJ gear in it and the rest of my clothes. I hooked the trailer up to the van, told my wife where I would be and left the house. That was Saturday, July 8th.

4

WHAT'S UP WITH ALL THIS CRYING?

~

I drove to the industrial park where the church and RV were, put some things in it and waited for church the next morning. I was now staying in the church parking lot with the RV, my van, my trailer, and everything I owned. I discussed my plans with Pastor Dorie and Jeff: to go to northern Arizona where this stone company was, to see about getting a job with their company, and to pray for my wife to let me come back home. I told them I would have to wait for a week because the owner of the stone company was in Colorado and couldn't see me until the following week. At least I had a plan for the next few weeks, but my heart was broken and confused. I kept thinking, "What are my girls and wife at home thinking? Do they think their father has abandoned them? Does my wife think I've lost my mind and will come to my senses soon?"

The first few days in the RV were incredibly hard. Daytime temperatures were 115 degrees and the RV air conditioning could not keep up. The temperature inside the RV was over 100 degrees until about four in the morning when it would finally dip below 90. My DJ gear and I were taking a beating and I was trying to hold it together, but I wasn't doing so well. I would call my friend Darryl each day to describe what I was going through, sharing with him the challenges with the heat and the RV.

Then one day Darryl called me and asked if I had heard about a large music festival that was going to be held in the state of

Washington. I told him it was on that list of events the Lord had given me. He then went on to tell me that he had gotten a call from a guy that was part of a national booking agency. This agency is one of the largest Christian agencies in the nation based out of New York and Nashville. This agent had heard of Darryl and was calling from New York to see if they could book him to play and do a seminar on using music and multimedia in the church today. The agent went on to tell Darryl they would pay him $5,000 to be at this huge festival in Washington, if he would perform. Darryl went on to tell the agent that he had retired from spinning and did not have the equipment he needed to do a multimedia seminar yet. Darryl explained that the necessary equipment would cost him around $5,000. He also told the agent that at this point, he had only raised $1,100 toward the gear he needed. The agent asked if he could call Darryl back the following week to see if they could work out something and Darryl agreed. Darryl later told me that the agent had said that the attendance at all Christian Festivals was way down and that they were trying to find a way to bring more people to these events. They thought that if they could give people something they could take back to their church they might be able to draw more people. Darryl asked me what I thought about their idea. I said, "Are they trying to market Jesus or invite people to a place to worship and have an encounter with Him?" Darryl explained that it's all about marketing. He said, "But the Lord doesn't need a PR person. He can take care of that himself." The Lord just needs people who will invite Him to dwell among them.

We talked for a while longer and then I turned my attention back to the situation at hand. The rest of the day I was thinking, "How am I going to cool this RV down enough for me to sleep at night and not toast my electronic gear?" The church had a back storage area with a loading bay roll-up door. Just maybe I could fit this 28-foot RV inside. It wasn't air conditioned, but at least I would be out of the sun during the day. I worked all day to move things around in order to squeeze the RV into the storage area. It fit by just inches. At least I could do that much.

It was now Friday, July 14th. I had been away from my house for a week and I was looking forward to meeting the owner of the stone company in northern Arizona and finding a way to get back into my house. I had planned on taking my portfolio of my stone designs to the stone company and was sure that after they had seen some of my pieces we would be able to work something out. That was *my* plan.

I was moving some things around in the RV later that day when I heard the Lord tell me that He wanted me to make a CD. I thought, "How am I going to pull this off?" Well, after some creative storage arrangements, I set up my DJ gear in the RV. I asked the Lord, "What do you want me to make this CD about?" He told me to make this CD about the King. So, I prayed about which worship songs the Lord wanted me to put on this CD. This was nothing new to me, as this was the way I made all the CD's the Lord had me produce over the years. Then the title and the theme of the CD came to me. The title was to be "Songs for My King". The recording of this CD was one of the most powerful and emotional times I have ever had playing for the Lord. I cried a lot during the process.

I know you are thinking, "Man, what's up with all the crying?" But the Lord says that He is close to the brokenhearted and I sure qualified in this category.

5

WHERE ARE YOU GOING?

~

On Saturday morning, I made several copies of this new CD and dropped them off to a few friends that I felt the Lord was leading me to bless. I brought some CDs to Darryl and talked to him about my next move to visit the stone company. The next day, Sunday the 16th, was my last Sunday at the Source Worship Center. The service was powerful as always. After service, Pastor Dorie and Pastor Jeff gave me some money to help me out. I thanked them and said I would call them after I got back from my appointment with the stone company. Then I called Darryl and told him that I had gotten an answer from the Lord on how to bring more people to the Christian Music Festivals around the country. I told Darryl, "I have been to these music festivals and enjoyed the Christian artists that perform, but none of these festivals have a 24/7 prayer and worship tent where people can go at anytime, day or night." Some of them have prayer tents but they are usually very small and hard to find compared with everything else that the festivals have to offer. From my own personal experience with such events and what I'd come across researching the upcoming summer music festivals, there seemed to be no 24/7-worship presence. We are created to love and to worship the Lord, yet that did not seem really high on the list of priorities for many Christian festivals. Even though they might have one or two worship services to offer people as a large group, it was usually only on the Sunday morning of the event.

I told Darryl that there is a hunger in the body of Christ for His presence. Darryl said that the next time he talked to the agent for the music festival in Washington, he would tell him what the Lord told me. As we talked some more, I told Darryl that I would like to have a prayer and worship tent at that music festival.

The next morning, July 17th, I left for my appointment with the stone company. It was a four-hour drive from Phoenix. I arrived at my appointment that afternoon only to find that the owner could not make it and had to reschedule for a date in another two weeks. I was invited to stay for the night at the stone company. They had a brand new travel trailer for guests who were from out of town and suggested I stay for the night.

The manager of the stone company and his wife invited me to dinner that night. After dinner, I showed the both of them the portfolio of my stone designs. They told me that they truly believed the owner of the company would be interested in hiring me after he took a look at my work. I stayed the night and the next day I thanked them for their hospitality. They assured me something big was going to happen for me soon. As I drove back to Phoenix, I was praying, "What next Lord?" A few months before, a stone company in Coeur d'Alene, Idaho, had contacted me. They were interested in my work. They had heard of me through my friends Kim and Jim and the work I was doing with their stone company in Phoenix. They had invited me to visit their company in Idaho anytime. So, as I was driving, I thought, "I will go back to Phoenix, get my trailer, hook it up to the van and head to Idaho."

First, I would need to get my tags on the van updated. I went to the department of motor vehicles and waited with the other five hundred people for my number to be called. When my turn came, I went up to the teller window with my paper- work and sat down at the table across from the teller. As he went through the papers that I handed to him and checked out the info on his computer, I commented on how beautiful and different the cross was that he wore around his neck. He stopped what he was doing and leaned close to me across the table, looking around to see if anyone was watching him. I leaned closer as he said, "You are a Christian, right?" I said, "Yes, I am. I have a multimedia ministry to preteens, teens and college students and for the past few years I've been working with the homeless and drug addicts on the streets." He looked me in the eyes and said, "Where are you going?" I thought that was a strange question to ask someone who was just getting his car tags renewed. I didn't answer right away. He told me it would be $400 for the tags. I wasn't expecting it to be that much, but I couldn't leave the state without them. So I gave him the money and then told him I was going to Coeur d'Alene, Idaho. He mentioned that he was familiar with the area and had moved to Phoenix from Seattle after having lived in Spokane for years. He explained that Spokane was not too far from Coeur d'Alene. Leaning forward again, he said, "I have some pastors you need to meet in Spokane." He again looked to his left and right and pulled open one of his desk drawers, taking out a small address book and writing down three names of people I was to call when I got to Spokane. I thanked him for his help and went on my way tucking the small piece of paper with the names and phone numbers into my wallet.

I went back to the RV happy about the connection we had just made. I unloaded everything from the RV and transferred it all into the van and my trailer. After filling both, I could see they were overloaded, but I had no choice. I had to make something happen and everything had to go with me. The RV was really too old to make the trip and I wasn't sure I could afford the gas to get there and back. It was over fifteen hundred miles from Phoenix to Coeur d'Alene.

I left Wednesday, July 19th, and went to stay the night in Cottonwood, Arizona, with a pastor friend and his family whom I had known for over sixteen years. He invited me to stay with them as long as I needed. I stayed with them until Thursday and then decided to stop by the stone company I had visited to check in one more time before heading on to Coeur d'Alene. On my way to the quarry, I got a call from my friend Darryl to let me know that he had had a conversation with the agent from New York about the large music festival in Washington. I could tell by Darryl's voice that he wasn't too happy. He told me that he had had a three-way conference call with the agent from New York and one of the top-booking agents in Nashville. They had told Darryl once again that they would like him to be a part of the Washington event, and again Darryl said that he didn't have the necessary equipment. Darryl told them he had $1,100 toward the $5,000 he needed. The agent from New York said he would personally give him $1,000. Again Darryl declined, but told them he had sent them a CD that his friend made. He explained to them, "The Lord told Bobby that what is missing at these festivals is a large worship tent open 24/7 during the festival." Darryl went on to tell them that I should be there. The agent from Nashville said, "Well is he nationally known?" Darryl told him, "Not yet." The agent pursued the conversation and went on to describe the different pay levels for artists and informed Darryl, "What it is really about is 'How many butts can he put in the seats'. If your friend wants a prayer tent at this festival in Washington, he will need to pay us $10,000 and provide an insurance rider for thirty million dollars in case he burns down the festival." Darryl told him that he didn't think I would do that. The agent also shared that the tent would only hold a few hundred people and this was a festival of 40,000 people. Darryl asked the agent if they would at least give me a ticket to the festival. The Nashville agent said, "No," and that I would have to buy my ticket to the festival like everyone else. Darryl told him, "Let me get this straight, you're willing to pay me $5,000 and you won't give my friend one complimentary ticket to check out this festival?"

After the Nashville agent hung up, Darryl talked to the agent from New York. During the whole conversation about a worship tent and me, the Nashville agent had never mentioned the Lord or the importance of worship at this event. The New York agent agreed that it was strange. Darryl said to me, "It's all about the money and marketing Jesus." He asked the New York agent to please listen to the CD that I had made called "Songs for My King." The agent promised that he would.

Darryl told me, "Bobby, you are to go to this event in Washington." Taken aback, I replied that I was now going to the stone company on my way to New Mexico, then through Colorado and up to Idaho to get to Coeur d'Alene. The route God was leading me on was already taking me by a round about road and this festival was in the middle of Washington State, not on my way to, or from, Coeur d'Alene. Again, Darryl said, "You have to go and show them what you do." I said, "If the Lord makes a way, then I'll go."

6

LET IT RAIN

~

Everyday I was just trying to hold it together. I would pray and ask the Lord to comfort my wife and children. How would any of this make sense to them? Had their father lost his mind chasing these crazy dreams? I would think about my wife, Cheryl, and her first marriage, how her husband became addicted to cocaine and would stay out partying for days and not come home. The pain of abandonment and the betrayal of his vow to only love her and my daughter, Kristyn, must have been terrible. Seeing all this when Kristyn was only three or four years old, I wondered if I was bringing another kind of pain on my wife and three children. As I was thinking about all of this, I got one of many extremely painful phone calls from my own mom. She called me and said, "Son, what are you doing? Why have you abandoned your family?" I said, "Mom, I haven't abandoned my family. I'm waiting to meet the owner of this stone company in northern Arizona and I am on my way to Coeur d'Alene to see the manager of a very large stone company." My mom told me, "You're making a big mistake leaving your family."

I knew where the pain was coming from in my mother's voice. My own father, who I am named after, left my mom and five children. He would abandon us for years at a time. His drug and alcohol addiction took over his life and he was never with us to help. There was almost an eighteen-year gap from the last time I saw him to the day my half brother called to say my father was dying in a Phoenix hospital and that he wanted to see me. At that time, I went home to tell my wife and she said, "Do you want us to go with you?" I said that I thought it would be better if she and the children did not see him this way. My father had not met my wife and children and I didn't want them to see him dying in the hospital bed. So, I brought a picture of my family to show him. I went to the hospital and made my way to his room to find my two half brothers and half sister along with their mom there, sitting next to my father. He had tubes coming out of his body. My half brother told me the doctors didn't think he would make it through the night. As my dad looked in my direction, tears came down his face. He had an oxygen mask on and was having a difficult time breathing. No words needed to be spoken in that moment. I could read his eyes. I held up the picture of my beautiful wife and three children and told him, "These are your grandchildren." Tears were streaming down his face. I came next to his bed and said, "Dad, there is no way you can give me back all the time lost between us, and my children want to know the answer to one question. Will we see grandpa in Heaven? So Dad, I'm asking you that question and don't screw with me. Dad, do you know Jesus Christ as your Lord and Savior?" My dad nodded yes, he did know Jesus. That was good enough for me. I held his hand and told him I loved him and then I left.

You might think, "Why did you need to know that?" My mother had been through so much pain because of my father, I couldn't even describe it. He would come home after being gone for months and years only to go out for milk one night and disappear for another eight years. He went all over the country, getting various jobs that fed his addictions, hardly ever returning home to his family. It wasn't his lack of love for his family that kept him from us; it was the alcohol and drugs. He was never totally set free. I believe it was on his deathbed that deliverance was finally made.

So, now my mom was reliving the pain of abandonment through her oldest son. My wife was reliving her five years of abandonment from her first husband and all I wanted to do was go home and make things right. The problem was that as each day my life became less of my will and more of the Lord's will, the less my family understood. I was now on my way to Coeur d'Alene, Idaho. I have two sisters that live there with their children. I was looking forward to seeing them. Both of my sisters knew what had been going on for the past few weeks and the younger of the two didn't want to talk to me. Memories of my father, and the reality of what I was doing, were bringing back the painful memories of our childhood to them and my mom. My other sister, who is just four years younger than me, said I could spend the night at her house. She was praying that I would get a job with the stone company and maybe be able to move my family there.

The journey to Coeur d'Alene was anything but easy. I slept in the van in a large chain store parking lot where I thought I would be safest. I was looking forward to getting to cooler temperatures and away from the Phoenix heat, but the strange thing was, as I traveled from Arizona to Idaho, every state and every city I went through was having a record heat wave. So as I drove I prayed, "Lord, everywhere that I have driven through and everywhere I'm about to go, let it rain. Bring water to the land and Your Spirit to Your thirsty children."

When I arrived in Coeur d'Alene, it was Sunday, July 23rd. I finally made it to my sister's house and was looking forward to sleeping in a bed and taking a hot shower. The next day I had an appointment with the stone company and then I decided I would visit Spokane to keep my promise to the man I met at the Department of Motor Vehicles in Phoenix. My appointment the next day went well. The general manager was impressed with my stone designs and work. He asked if I would be interested in moving to Coeur d'Alene. I told him that if the price was right, maybe I would. He said, "I have your phone number. I'll get back to you."

I returned to my sister's home and told her what happened and explained that I was now going to Spokane, Washington to meet some people and then I would be off to a Christian music festival there. I knew my sister thought I was crazy and probably wondered why I wasn't going straight back home. What I didn't tell her was that I was almost completely broke with no way to make it home. The overly packed van and trailer had given me less than half the mileage I thought I would get on this journey. After I said goodbye to my sister, I pulled out that small paper still in my wallet with the three names I was to call when I got to Spokane. I called all three. One pastor was no longer with the same church as before and promised to pray for me. The other pastor didn't answer, and the third was an elderly man, full of life and excitement. He asked if I could meet him at a Starbucks close to his house. He gave me directions and I told him I would meet him the next day at 10:00 A.M.

7

CAN YOU SING?

~

Every couple of days I would call home to my wife and children. My wife really didn't want me to speak to my children. They were hurt and confused. I would think of them all day, every day. I knew my mother and father-in-law wouldn't understand either, and the thought of them in pain, over me seemingly abandoning my family, was too much to think about along with everyone else. I kept thinking to myself, I'm not on vacation; I'm on an assignment from the Lord.

The next morning, I drove to Spokane and arrived half an hour early. I went into Starbucks, got one of my favorite coffee drinks and went outside to wait for someone I had never met. I just smiled at everyone and at about 10:00 A.M. an elderly gentleman in his 80's walked up to me with a Bible in his hand and said "Good Morning, Bobby." He told me his name and I asked if I could buy him some coffee. He told me, "No, thank you. I'll get it." He went inside Starbucks, got some coffee, came back out and sat down. He said, "So, tell me about the journey the Lord has taken you on so far." I went on to tell him about the past few weeks and that I didn't understand everything the Lord was doing, but I had come this far and knew I had to go on. He said, "Our life here on earth is an amazing journey when the Lord is truly Lord over our lives." He told me to go all the way. He opened up his Bible and read a scripture that the Lord had given him just for me that morning. I really felt like I was sitting in the presence of a great man of God. He told me his wife was sick with cancer and he missed their ministry times together so much. I asked, "What do you mean?" He said, "We used to go to the prisons together to minister to the inmates." He stated that she would go there for the ladies and he would pray and intervene for her in the car and she would do the same for him when he ministered to the men. He told me he could only go once a month now because of her health. He went on to tell me that now they let him minister to those on death row. I asked, "Through the glass?" He said yes. I paused for a moment and looked him in his eyes. I could feel this overwhelming presence of the Lord as I asked him, "Can you sing?" He just stared at me as I asked him again. There was a long pause as his eyes welled up with tears. "Are you allowed to teach them worship songs and sing to them?" I inquired. He said, "Bobby, I perceive that the Lord has directed you to ask me this question." He started to cry as he told me that the Lord had been asking him to teach the men in prison how to worship Him. They might never be released from prison and the bars that kept them there, but if they could learn to worship Him, the chains that keep them bound in their hearts and minds would be broken off. He told me that the Lord had asked him many times to do this and he had told the Lord each time, "I'm too old and my voice is not what it used to be." He stated that he used to have a beautiful singing voice but his voice had now become "crackly," as he put it.

He looked at me and said, "I promise you, Bobby, I will do what the Lord is asking me to do through you. Maybe He sent you all the way from Phoenix, Arizona because I wouldn't listen." He reached in his coat pocket and pulled out his checkbook and said, "Your ministry is good soil and I'm going to plant a seed in this soil." He wrote me a check for fifty-six dollars and said, "You will need this when the time comes and I trust you will know when." We talked some more and laughed and cried together. I thought, "Lord, thank you for bringing him into my life. Bless him and heal his wife." At the end of our time together, he told me, "I'll be hearing about you one day, Bobby. Keep fighting for this generation of young people. They are the last ones." We hugged and I said goodbye. I got into the van, looked at the map of Washington State and said to myself, "I guess I'm going to the music festival in Washington after all."

8

FESTIVAL OR BUST

~

I went to put gas in the van and started to figure whether or not I had enough money to make it to the festival and how much I would have left over for food. The festival wasn't until the next day, so if I could get there I would park my van, sleep in the van and pray that someone had an extra ticket they could give me so that I could get in. I looked at the map again. I had a few hundred miles to drive, so I started on my way. I called Darryl, explained my plans and told him I would call him when I got to the festival.

A few hours later, I arrived in a small town about twenty miles from the festival. The festival would last for five days and I would need food. As I got out of the van, I thought the trailer looked tilted closer to my bumper than I'm used to seeing. When I looked closer I noticed two cracks in the tube frame of the trailer. They ran more than halfway through the tubing. I just stood there and stared. This could snap off at anytime and the trailer would go off tumbling down the freeway, possibly taking me with it. What was I going to do? I was 1,500 miles from home and it wasn't like I could simply call for help from friends or family. To them I had lost my mind, abandoned my family and I was chasing a dream that I would never catch. The whole time I was thinking, "Lord, what am I doing?" Again I heard the words, "Keep going, there will be plenty of time to cry." Great! With that in mind, I simply decided to not worry about the tubing and just continue to follow God's lead.

It had been over a week since I had talked to Pastor Dorie or Pastor Jeff. They had no idea where I was, but if I did tell them, I knew they would come to my rescue in a minute. That is just the kind of people they are. I felt that the Lord, however, was not letting me talk to them yet. I was grateful that I could talk to Darryl almost every day and let him know what was going on.

I was now twenty miles from the Gorge Amphitheater where the large music festival was to be held. It was Tuesday, July 25th. I had been out the house for seventeen days. Later, as I carefully drove down the dirt road that lead to the amphitheater, I called Darryl to tell him I was close. I had been the only one on the road for a while, but when some cars pulled up behind me I decided to pull over and try to figure out what to do. I wanted to get close enough to the festival to be able to park along the road and wait until morning. Darryl had suggested making a sign in the morning that read, "Need ticket!" Someone was bound to give me one or buy me one, he thought. He had been going to and playing at music festivals for years and many people had just enough to get there and then pray for a ticket, some holding up signs outside the festival hoping to get in.

As I was talking to Darryl, more and more cars began passing by and I thought, "The festival doesn't start until tomorrow, where are they going?" When I got off the phone, I started following the cars that went by. We started picking up speed and I became excited. I saw vans and cars with the 'name-of-the-festival or bust' all over them, in front and behind me. I was going the right way! As we traveled down the road, we came to what I would later find out was a checkpoint. There was a man on the side of the road waving cars on. As I went by, he excitedly waved at me. I thought, man that guy was really nice. Maybe he was excited to see me, and my trailer. I had graphics all over the trailer and Not of This World Productions (my production logo) on the front and back. As the cars picked up speed, my heart raced a bit. What in the world was waiting around the corner? Just then we made the turn and there on the hillside were hundreds of cars, vans, RVs, and trailers. A long line formed as the festival volunteers directed people into lanes that were marked off with colored stakes and flags. I was directed to pull right behind a van full of college students. As I stopped a few feet from them, I looked down the hill in the direction of hundreds of cars, bumper-to-bumper, coming into the festival. I got out of the van and took a deep breath. I thought, "I'm in! I can't believe it!" As people parked their vehicles and started to come out, there was an amazing atmosphere of anticipation and joy. I could hear people talking to friends they had known for years as they walked through the sea of vehicles. I called Darryl back to tell him, "I'm in!"

9

TELL THEM WHO YOU ARE

~

It was getting close to sunset and people were pulling out their portable grills and the smell of food was everywhere. I thought I should probably eat as well and I heard the Lord say, "Do not worry about food. They will bring food before you. Eat and bless those who feed you." The Lord also told me, "Wherever you go, don't worry, I'll take care of you. Do not store up anything extra. Just bless those who bless you." Just then the college students in front of me asked if I would like to come over and eat with them. They were having hot dogs and hamburgers and had more than enough. I grabbed my camping chair and joined them. They asked me about my van and trailer and what my ministry was all about. They said, "We saw your license plates are from Arizona. You are a long way from home. Where do you live?" I told them that, yes, I was from Phoenix, Arizona and that the Lord had sent me to this festival. I asked if this was their first time here. They told me that they had been coming to this festival for many years and were from a town a few hours away in Washington. It was great to fellowship with them as they laughed and joked with each other. They asked what I had in my trailer. I told them it held all of my sound gear, television monitors, a generator, and a ton of other things. They asked if I would be playing at the festival and doing worship since there was a tent that was having seminars and speakers discussing worship. I told them that if the Lord opened that door then I would be there.

After spending some time with them, the people from the truck behind me came over to ask some questions about my trailer and what had brought me to this festival. I shared with them my desire to bring worship to music festivals that people could be a part of 24/7 while the festival was going on. They loved the idea and shared that they thought it was great to come to the festival to see and hear the different Christian artists, but they had a deep hunger for the presence of God and wanted to join in more worship with others who had the same hunger. They always left the festival encouraged and blessed, but they also felt that there was something missing. I asked if it was an undistracted encounter with God that was missing and they both looked at me and replied, "Yes." What was lacking was somewhere they could worship Him as long as they wanted to, no matter what time, day or night. "Why is there nothing like that?" they asked. I told them that I had suggested the idea, but I had been shot down from entering the front door of this festival. But maybe God was bringing me through the back door.

About this time one of the volunteer workers was coming around to check out the reservation cards on the dashboards of each vehicle. As he came to check the people I had just been talking to, they showed him a large card on the dashboard of their car. I finally realized why that man at the checkpoint was waving at me when I came in. Every vehicle had one of those cards clearly visible. The volunteer worker scanned their card and came over to me and asked if I had a pre-registration card that he could see. As I watched him checking the other cars, I was thinking, Lord what do You want me to do. He said, "Tell them who you are." I told the guy I was DJ Bobby D from Phoenix, Arizona and was supposed to be doing worship here at the festival and that I had not received a pre-registration card. He said that he would talk to his supervisor to see if my name was left at Will Call. He promised they would get back to me soon. After he left, some of the people around me told me this was just a pre-staging area and at midnight everyone would be moving into the lower camping area right next to the festival grounds. I watched as thousands of cars, vans and RVs were being staged all over the hillside and there I was, right in the middle of it. About half an hour later the supervisor for the festival grounds came by to see me. I gave him my Not of this World Productions card and said I was supposed to be doing worship at the festival. He said that Will Call wasn't open yet and asked if I wanted to be moved to where the other artists for the festival were; they would move me down there right away. I told him that I enjoyed being with the people that were attending the festival and that there was no need to move me. He said he would have someone bring over my registration card for my vehicle and a wristband to get me into the festival. I thanked him. The people that I was talking to before were standing right beside the supervisor the whole time we were having this conversation. After he left, the wife looked at me and said, "I guess the Lord wants you here Bobby." I replied, "I guess He does. I just wish my family was here with me."

10

GO! GO!

~

As I looked around I saw there were hundreds of families everywhere. Some people from a few rows of vehicles away came over to talk. They had heard about me from their friends and asked if I could play some music while everyone was waiting until midnight to be moved. I told them I would have to get my gear out of the trailer and they offered to help. I pulled out my equipment and generator. All the vehicles were parked close together with about five feet between each row of vehicles. I hooked everything up but when I went to start my generator, it wouldn't work. I thought, "This is strange; it always starts with one pull." I tried for ten minutes, but with no luck. Once again, the campers that were right behind me came to the rescue. They pulled out their generator and fired it up. It was a different brand than mine and much quieter. As it started to get dark, I put up rope lights around my gear so people wouldn't fall over the equipment and then I started to play worship music for those around me as well those down the hill. What I hadn't thought about was that I was the only one with a sound system and that I was at the very top of the hill. As I played the music, people from everywhere started coming around, setting up their camping chairs and singing along with the worship music. There were hundreds of people all around me and many of them were on their faces in the grass. I watched as people kept coming closer to worship. There were so many that they were actually tripping over those that were worshiping on their faces. It was beautiful to see the hunger and heart for God's presence.

I played for about an hour and a half and then I had to quickly pack up. We were going to move at midnight and it was now 11:30 P.M. Everyone helped put things away and we finished with about five minutes to spare. They started to move the rows one at a time and formed all the vehicles into one huge line leading into the lower camping area. Just then I remembered that no one had come back with my registration for my vehicle and my pass to the festival. Once again they were checking everyone's vehicles and I was next. They asked me where my registration was and I told them that they should call it in. I gave them the supervisor's name and they radioed him. Now I was holding up the entire festival line. The guy on the radio told me, "You are DJ Bobby D, aren't you?" I answered yes. He said that he had heard me playing music on the hill. I was thinking, "If they don't let me in, my Christian brothers and sisters in these thousands of cars behind me are going to wring my neck." But finally the call came back from the supervisor to get me in. The guy that I was talking to yelled for someone to run to the tent to get me a registration card. By now, all the vehicles that had been in front of me were totally out of sight. The man came back over to my van and gave me a registration card, slapped a green sticker on my windshield and said, "Go, go!" I took off, but realized too late that they hadn't given me a wristband to get into the festival. But that would have to be a problem to resolve later.

As I headed down the hill, I passed through a maze of volunteers directing which way to go. I finally caught up to the line and they were conducting the single campers, tents and groups to one area and the RVs and travel trailers to another. As I approached the workers, they looked at the green sticker on my van and instructed, "You have to follow the campers with the tents." I heard the Lord say, "Follow the RVs." So, I said, "I have to go with the RVs." They replied, "Sir, we can't let you." I explained, "I'm going to be doing worship at the festival and need to be with the RVs." So they let me pass and I was directed to park in a space next to a large RV with a boat. Then a travel trailer came and parked on the other side of me. I couldn't believe it. I was finally in; at least I could camp now.

It was now around 1:00 A.M. and as I looked up on the hill, there were still thousands and thousands of vehicles coming into the festival. Some people next to me said it would be like this until 6:00 A.M. I was so exhausted. I went back to the van and sat down. I closed my eyes and listened as thousands of campers were setting up their camps. It was amazing. I couldn't sleep, so I just sat there until the sun came up at 6:30 A.M. When I got out of the van and looked around, all I could see in every direction were tents, trailers, RVs, cars, etc. The first concerts would start about midday and people everywhere were continuing to set up their areas. Each camping section was divided by rows that were about two car lengths wide. It was designed very efficiently and comfortably to allow plenty of room for foot traffic on the other side of the section. I was camping close to where about twenty porta-potties were located. I thought, "Well, this is an interesting place you have put me, Lord, because everyone will be in this area using the porta-potties at one time or another." As I continued to take the scene in, the people from next door with the RV and the boat came over and introduced themselves and asked if I would join them for breakfast. I thanked them for the invitation and grabbed my camping chair once again. They told me they were from Canada and had been coming to this festival for the past few years. They had four children. Three of them were teenagers and the youngest was twelve. They had noticed I was a DJ and asked me about my trailer. I explained that I was from Phoenix, Arizona and that the Lord had sent me to this festival. The mother then asked me if I was by myself or if my family would be joining me. I said that they were still back in Phoenix. "So," she said, "you are all by yourself on this journey."

I thought to myself, "There is that word again, 'Journey.'" I had a hard time looking her straight in the eyes. I knew she could see and feel my pain. She said, "Bobby, you are welcome to join us anytime and we will take care of you and feed you." I thanked her for her and her family's hospitality. I explained that I did have plenty of food and water, but that I would love to eat and fellowship with them whenever they would have me. I felt truly blessed.

11

CAPTIVE AUDIENCE

~

That morning the camp was buzzing with activity all around as by the hundreds people passed by my campsite on their way to the main entrance to the festival. My new friends asked if I was going to see any of the Christian artists in concert today. I told them I would probably see some later, so they took off with their camping chairs, water and blankets and headed inside with the rest of the crowd. I decided to set up my 10 x 10 easy-up shade tent behind my trailer. I sat in the shade of my tent and prayed, "Okay Lord, I'm in the camping area, now what?" I didn't get an answer right away, so I continued to wait. A few hours later, my Canadian friends came back to have lunch. They had visited two stages and seen some of their favorite artists and they told me about how great the concerts had been. As they prepared lunch, they asked me how I was doing and I told them I had been relaxing and praying. After awhile their youngest son came over and said, "Bobby, mom says lunch is ready." So I ate with them again and enjoyed the food and fellowship. After lunch they headed back for the afternoon concerts and told me they would catch up with me later.

In the afternoon, temperatures got over one hundred degrees and people were drinking as much water as they could. It seemed like everyone had portable generators to run their trailers and the air conditioning units in them. As I sat in the shade, the father of the family on the other side of my campsite came over and introduced himself. His name was Brent. He and his family were also Canadian but from an area hundreds of miles away from my new friends. They had brought a large travel trailer and had two small children. When they mentioned the heat, I told them that I was from Phoenix and even at midnight it would still be 100°. They asked, "How could you live in that heat?" I told them it was possible only with air conditioning and high-energy bills. After inviting me to join him and his family later, he asked if I was traveling alone and I replied that I was. Brent asked, "Are you going to the concerts tonight?" I told him that I might, but was not sure yet. When evening came around, both families brought me dinner. I did not turn either one down, as I remembered what the Lord told me: "Eat whatever is set before you and bless those who feed and take care of you."

That evening everyone headed to the concerts. The main stage was set in a huge amphitheater. I could sometimes hear the music, but only just enough to tease me into wanting to go. Later, as everyone was coming back, they shared with me stories of their experiences and the fun they had had. Then they went back to their RVs, trailers, and tents. I pulled out my air mattress and sleeping bag and laid it down on the ground to sleep. I asked the Lord, "What do you want me to do here?" Still no answer.

I woke up early, around six in the morning; it was now Thursday, July 27th. There were people moving around at their campsites but there was no one walking down the road yet. After I put away my sleeping bag and mattress, I noticed this older lady in her 70's walking up one of the roads toward me. She had her hands extended toward each side of the road where the campsites were laid out. She walked toward me, smiled, and turned to use the portable potties. When she came out, she looked at me, smiled, and went down the road toward the entrance of the festival with her arms outstretched like a bird flying. I watched her as she disappeared down the hill. I asked the Lord again, "What do you want me to do?" Finally, He answered, "Set up your equipment and play to all those who come by and who can hear you in their campsites." I said, "OK, Lord."

The four kids from my Canadian friends next door came over and said, "Bobby, Mom says breakfast is ready." We ate together again as they planned out their music schedule for the day. All four kids took off with great excitement with their father following along. I helped their mom clean up and she asked me to sit down awhile and talk. So, I did.

She asked me how I had gotten to the festival and about my family. I told her everything that had happened up to that day. I missed my family so much and my heart broke as I recounted the events of the past few weeks. As I was crying, she told me, "God is looking for obedient servants to do His will. God will help take care of your family and heal your marriage, as you are obedient to Him." I told her that I didn't know what to tell my wife, family, and friends. How could I tell them that I was at a Christian concert, 1,500 miles away, waiting for God to tell me what my next move was? I didn't think that that would go over too well, considering my wife was struggling to pay our bills and take care of our children while I was off traveling to music festivals. She again reassured me that the Lord was in control and to follow His leading. She looked at me again and asked, "Is the Lord going to let you see any of these artists while you are here?" I told her, "No!" My assignment was to minister to those around me and those who came by my campsite. She said, "I thought so. You don't even have a bracelet to get in, do you?" I said no. She asked, "Do you want us to get you one?" I thanked her but replied that I didn't need one. I figured that if the Lord wanted me inside the festival He would have provided a way by now. She said, "So, what will you do today?" I told her that I would set up my gear and play music for everyone from right where I was at until they kicked me out. I had nothing to lose and nowhere to go. She laughed, and I started laughing with her. I hadn't laughed for weeks and it felt good.

I started pulling all my gear out of my trailer: my generator, DJ gear, speakers, tables and extra camping chairs. As I was setting my gear up under the tent, a man walked over to me and introduced himself as Al. He asked about my ministry and where I was from. He was from a small town in Oregon and came to the festival with his teenage son. He said his teenage daughter was also there but had driven to the festival with her friends. She was sixteen and at that age where her father wasn't cool anymore. I laughed and I told him that I knew what he meant, myself having a sixteen year old at home in Phoenix. He asked, "Are you going to play music later?" I told him that I would play as soon as I was set up. He said, "My daughter sings and plays guitar and my son plays drums. He brought his conga drums with him. Can he come over to meet you?" I told him, sure. When I had everything set up, I hooked up the power to my generator, but once again the generator wouldn't start. I was thinking, "What a battle!" Just then Brent came over from his travel trailer. He said, "Let me look at the generator." Brent had a farm in Canada and was used to working on all his machinery. As he cleaned the spark plugs, the gas line and a few other things he said, "I'm sure with a little time, I can fix it." Until then, he offered his generator for me to use. He explained that he had borrowed it from a friend and liked it because of how quiet it was. I thanked him and I was now good to go.

By then it was around 9:00 A.M. I started playing worship music and watched the people passing by as they headed to the concerts by the hundreds. I enjoyed seeing people singing along with the music I was playing as they walked by. I pointed one of my speakers directly at the twenty or so porta-potties across the road from me. I figured I had a captive audience in the bathrooms. I laughed as people would come out of the bathroom and give me the thumbs up sign, before heading off to the concerts. It wasn't long until I saw the lady from the day before come by. This time she was walking up the road singing to the music I was playing. She smiled at me and kept going. Al's son came over with his congas and set them up right in front of the table with my DJ gear. I hooked up a small mixing board into my DJ board so I could mix live sound. I also set up two microphones on stands and put out a couple of camping chairs. As Al's son was jamming on the congas to what I was playing, soon people began stopping by and joining in singing. Al's daughter showed up about an hour later and asked me if she could sing and play her guitar. I said sure. She left to grab her guitar and I set up a microphone for her. She came back with her songbook of worship songs and sat down to play. As she started singing, I was amazed at how truly talented she was. Her brother joined in on the conga drums and now I had my own mini stage set up. People who were walking by on their way to the festival entrance would stop and stay to listen and sing with her. Al stood next to me and said, "What do you think?" I told him that they were great. What I loved most about the both of them was that they were lost in praising and worshipping the Lord. They didn't pay attention to anyone around them. They weren't distracted at all.

It wasn't long after that that a boy came by and, sitting in one of the camping chairs that I had put out, started singing with Al's daughter.

She looked over at him and smiled. He sang beautifully. She stopped playing the guitar and asked his name. He told her and asked if he could borrow her guitar for a minute. He promised that he would be careful with the instrument and explained that his dad was a musician. As he started playing the guitar, all those gathered around were shocked. He was awesome. And then he started singing. Al's daughter said, "How did you get so good?" He explained that he had been playing and singing since he was four years old and that he also played keyboards and drums. She asked him, "How many songs do you know?" He answered that he knew over 1,000. He had a photographic memory. I just looked around at the half dozen astonished faces as he played a few more songs, both old and new. He handed the guitar back to Al's daughter and just started singing along with her as she sang.

Brent came around the corner of his trailer to see what was up. He smiled at me and said he would be right back. Ten minutes later, Brent returned with another man holding a guitar and said, "Bobby, this is my friend, Tom. He is also from Canada and has a ministry called, 'Guitar Church' where he teaches people how to play the guitar online." Tom sat in for a few minutes while Al's daughter and the rest of the crowed worshipped together. Then Tom joined them on his guitar. The next thing I knew, three more young people came by to sit in the grass and worship. One young man in his twenties brought out his Bible and started to share from the Word of God. He had a cowboy hat on and told me he was from a small ranch in Oregon. Everyone stopped singing, but Tom kept playing his guitar quietly while the young man preached to us and encouraged us in the Lord. I was still amazed as he finished his message and joined everyone in once again worshipping the Lord. Then, from across the road, came two more college age guys with their guitars to join in. As more people came by on their way to the concerts, they would stop for a few minutes and join in on the worship. It was exciting for me to watch as the Lord brought together this group of worshipers. After a few hours had passed, everyone got ready to go to the concerts. After lunch, Brent said, "Don't worry about the generator, Bobby. I have plenty of gas." So I just kept playing worship music all day and through the evening.

12

THEY ARE THE LAST ONES

~

Early the next morning, Al brought breakfast to me. I waited until 8 A.M. to fire up the generator and start up the worship music for the day. Again, I saw the same older lady that I had seen every day so far walking up and down the road with her arms outstretched and praying. I could never quite make out what she was saying. It was now Friday and once again everyone came by to do worship, bringing their instruments with them. It was fun to watch them pray and worship together. Every once in a while a golf cart with festival credentials would drive by and wave at me. Well, I guess I was here to the end. That afternoon, I brought out my bigger speakers and played all the rest of the day and through to night. I talked to hundreds of people that day and was exhausted when it came time to shut down.

The following morning, Saturday, July 29th, I once again turned the generator on at 8:00 A.M. and started playing worship music. I watched as once more the elderly lady came up the road with arms outstretched, praying. I also had seen her around 6:00 A.M. walking and praying. She came right up to me and introduced herself. She said, "I want to thank you for being obedient to the Lord. You have bathed this area with worship music and music for the young people all day, every day." I said, "Can I ask you a question? I see you every morning walking up and down these roads between the tents, trailers and everywhere else, and you have your arms outstretched to each side of the road. What are you doing?" She told me she had been sent to this festival from her church, which was on the coast close to Seattle.

Everyone in her little church was old and they were ready to hand it over to this younger generation. She said, "They are the last ones."

There was that saying again. This was something that I had been saying and had been on my heart for years and now a stranger was telling me something that I knew to be true. She said, "Bobby, I walk up and down these roads with my arms outstretched and I pray that God would raise up an army of young people to walk in His Strength, Power and the Truth of His Word. I pray that this generation would rise up and take their place in the Kingdom of God and that He would call them and anoint them for the work of the Gospel. I pray that He would bring them to our town that we may pass the baton on to them. For our time is coming to an end." As I looked into her eyes, I could feel the Love of Christ coming right out of her. I said to her, "Thank you for your faithfulness to what the Lord has asked you to do." She smiled and looked at me and said, "And you, too." With those last words, she turned and headed down the road with her arms outstretched, praying as she went.

13

KEEP GOING

~

So many of my favorite Christian artists had performed at this festival and I didn't get to see a single one of them. But the next morning was filled with new friends and worship again. I remember two ladies in their mid 40's who came by to watch and listen to the young people. One woman came up to me and said, "They are incredible. I'm a praise and worship leader at my church and this is amazing." She asked me how old the boy was that was playing the guitar and singing. I told her that he was twelve years old and that he knew over a thousand different songs, including hymns that were centuries old. She stood there with her mouth open in awe. She asked, "Do you think they will let me join them?" I said sure. She said, "I'll be right back." She and her friend came back a few minutes later. She asked the group if they knew a particular song and started to sing and play the guitar. Everyone watched as she sang. Her voice was beautiful and had so much control. As everyone sat there listening, she invited them to join in as well. It was another Divine connection for all there as they sang and fellowshipped with each other, Canadians, Americans, Brothers and Sisters in Christ. It was really something to be right in the middle of it.

Later they all headed for the festival's last day of concerts and that afternoon the Lord told me to give away some of my equipment that I had brought with me. When everyone came back for lunch, I asked Al and his son if they could come over and help me with some things. When they came over to my trailer, I told them that the Lord had told me to give them some gear. I told Al, "This is for you because you have such a servant's heart." I gave him a complete sound system with speakers, a sixteen channel mixing board, amps and equalizer- the works. It was given to me by my friends Kim and Jim and had cost them thousands of dollars. I also gave Al a brand new karaoke system I had just bought and had used at a wedding my friends had asked me to play for. Lastly, I gave him a 27" high-end TV monitor for his karaoke system. Al was in tears. It was exactly what they had been praying for to have for the youth in his town. They could use the sound system to minister on the Indian Reservation where they had just built a new relationship. Al said, "I don't know what to say." I told him there was no need to say anything and, "Let's load this into your travel trailer," because I had more things to give away.

The Lord has always told me to be on the lookout for a place to plant seed. Al, his children, and their ministry to youth in their town, was good soil to plant seed. After we were done, I went to get Brent from his travel trailer and brought him to where my generator was. I told him what I had given to Al as Al and his son stood beside me. Then I told Brent, "The Lord told me to give you this generator." I looked at Brent. Even hidden behind his sunglasses I could see tears coming down his face. I said, "Brent, you have a hard time receiving things from people don't you?" He nodded his head yes. I said, "Brent, you are an awesome man of God and you help all those around you, don't you?" Again, he nodded yes. "God wants to bless you with this generator and you could use it, couldn't you?" He nodded yes yet again as tears came down his face. "This generator was given to me by a good friend of mine in Phoenix and if the Lord wants me to have a new one, He will get me one. I want to thank you and your family for feeding me and for your friendship and hospitality toward me." Brent gave me a hug and hugged Al and his son and then we loaded the generator into the back of his truck.

The festival was ending that night after a huge last act, and thousands of people would be heading out afterwards while the rest had to be gone by 10 the next morning. Al asked me when I would be leaving and I told him that I planned to head out in the morning. He said he would bring over some coffee before we left. That night I said good-bye to everyone. They would all be heading home and I was trying to figure out how in the world the Lord was going to get me back to my home. I had talked to Darryl a couple of days earlier. He had called and said, "Bobby, I just got an email about an event in Traverse City, Michigan. It's just the kind of event you've been waiting for the past sixteen years. All the top Christian DJs and DJs that play positive music will be there. There are going to be over sixty DJs from the U.S. and around the world. You have to go. It's August 25th – 27th." I replied, "Darryl, I have to go home, get a job and see if my wife will give me another chance. I also promised my friend, Pastor Greg, I would go to his youth camp in August in Northern Arizona and another Pastor's camp in Window Rock, AZ on the Navajo Reservation in September. I promised to go to these camps long before my wife asked me to leave." Darryl said, "God will make a way for you to go." I told him that it would take a miracle just to get me home, 1,500 miles away.

Sunday morning came and Brent and Al came by to bring me coffee. Al and his son brought over some nice hats they had bought for me from the festival and gave me twenty dollars. He said, "I know it's not much." I told Al it was perfect and asked him to call me sometime. I got into my van and felt the pain of being alone again. The Lord said, "Keep going, I am with you." With the money that Al had given me, I had about forty dollars and I still had all the food and water I had bought before the festival. The questions were whether or not I could make it to the nearest gas station and how was I going to fix my trailer? I headed back out onto the dirt road with the hundreds of other cars leaving that day. Mercifully, I made it to the gas station. I put all I had in the gas tank, took out my U.S. atlas and planned the shortest way to get back to Phoenix.

14

HAPPYTOWN

~

"Well," I thought, "with forty dollars in gas, I won't get far." It seemed clear that I was to go as far as I could and trust God to make a way from there. I got to Richland, Washington and pulled into a grocery store parking lot. I sat in the van and thought, "Who am I going to call for help?" It was obvious that God was not letting Darryl send me money. He was interceding for me and that was all God was letting him do. Pastor Dorie and Pastor Jeff didn't even know that I had left the state and God wasn't letting me call them. All of a sudden, I remembered the fifty-six dollar check from my friend in Spokane and his words to me, "You will know when to use it." The low fuel light was on in my van; that meant I would only go twenty miles before I was completely out of gas. I looked for a check-cashing store and found one a couple of blocks away. I cashed the check and put fifty in the gas tank. I took out the map and I said to the Lord, "I will go as far as this gas takes me and trust you again from there."

I made it all the way to Baker City, Oregon just as the low fuel light came on once again. I pulled off the freeway into the town. I stopped at a motel right off the exit ramp with a huge lot where the big-rigs and other trucks parked. I thought, "I will find the center of this town and park there." I drove about a mile into town and found a beautiful park with huge trees. There was an old-fashioned gazebo and picnic tables everywhere. At one end there was a river that ran through town and a bridge over the river that led to a public library. The park was bordered by homes on two sides, so I parked my van in front the houses and walked across the street. I was thinking about my next step and how I would be able to continue on my journey, when my mind kept going back to one of the big-rigs that I had seen just a few blocks away. It was one of those rigs that was pulling another trailer. I think they are called doubles. I'm not a truck driver, but I think that's what they are called. Anyway, I was thinking to myself, "why is this double parked so close to the park and this residential area when all the other big trucks are parked next to the freeway?" The other thing that was strange was that it was a truck representing a name brand potato chip company. I had passed the grocery stores to get to this area and here was this truck, just sitting right next to the park. Finding no immediate answer to my thoughts, I decided to call Darryl to give him an update and let him know where I was. I told him, "I don't know why God has stopped me in this town." Darryl said, "Who's in the park?" I told him, "Just one guy sitting on a park bench eating a sandwich." As I was talking to Darryl, the man with the sandwich got up, threw the rest of his sandwich in the trash and walked across the park toward my van and trailer. I told Darryl, "I will call you later. God is up to something." The man walked up to my trailer and stood on the sidewalk. He was reading the poem that was on three sides of my trailer. The poem reads as follows:

HAPPYTOWN

Everyone wants to live in Happytown.

No pain, No fear, No death, No Hell.

Everyone wants a house with a white picket fence

No rain, No floods, No break-ins, No fire.

Everyone wants a perfect little world

No war, No dictators, No bombs, No Army.

Every man wants a perfect woman,

No blemishes, Blonde hair, Blue eyes, nice tan.

Every woman wants a perfect man,

Nice job, New car, Good money, Strong face.

No one ever wakes up in Happytown

Because it doesn't exist in this world.

Down here it's not so perfect,

People bleed, People cry, People break down.

Yet, everyone chases a vision

Ignoring....

Always ignoring the only Perfection

There is a town called HOPE.

Deep in the heart

Ruled by a King

Open to all...

The door is a Son

The City is real

By Steve M.

I stood next to the man and asked, "What do you think?" He said, "This is so true. I was eating my sandwich over in the park and looked over at your trailer and something pulled me over here to read this." I asked, "Do you live here?" He answered, no, that he was a route driver for a big potato chip company. The company had told him that they had made a mistake in his mileage route and that he would need to stay in Baker City overnight. In all his years as a driver, this had never happened to him. He said that had he called his wife the night before to tell her what was going on. So, I said, "Is that your big rig truck just down the road?" He said yes. He had gotten a sandwich for lunch and was going to leave right after he ate and that is when he saw my van and trailer. I began to tell him, "About fifteen years ago, I helped produce and engineer a radio show in Phoenix called Radio Hope and one of the contributing writers who had written some incredible poetry for the people on the streets, wrote that poem and it became sort of a signature for our two hour radio show. My friend had said I could use the poem however I wanted. So, one of the ways I chose was to put it on my trailer. It would take all day to tell you about the people who have read this poem and their responses." He asked me, "The plates on your trailer say Arizona. What part of Arizona are you from?" I told him Phoenix. He said, "What are you doing here?" I gave him the 15-minute story. He looked at me and said, "Bobby, it is so good to meet someone who loves Christ and is doing something about it. I'm sure the trials and struggles you and your family have gone through have been really hard, but I believe God is going to use this for His glory." I also told him that I had made it to this town with about two dollars in change left. He asked me an interesting question. He said, "Bobby, do you believe the church of America is effective in reaching the youth of today?" I said, "No, but that is about to change. This is the last generation, I believe the Lord is stirring His church and shaking it. There are people in churches today who can't take it anymore. They love God and are hungry for God and all they are getting is man's program of what they think God should do." He started to get big tears in his eyes. He told me that right before he had left home for this trip, he and his wife had decided to leave their church of nine years. They were tired of the pastors and leaders spending all this money on what he called "Their Kingdom," "Their Programs," "Their Buildings," and nothing for the youth and those that wanted to do more to reach people. He told me that he and his wife loved God but were so disillusioned with the church. I told him, "We are the church. Ask the

Lord what you can do to help. Love others and pray that God would move on the hearts of the pastors and leaders. Better yet, ask if you could pray for them, and with them, for the church." I continued, "The Harvest is big and the workers are ready. That means you and me."

The whole time I was talking to him, he was crying. He said, "Bobby, do you believe in Divine Appointments?" I kind of laughed and said, "Yes, I do." He told me that he believed we were having one right now. He said, "I will be praying for you," and then he turned and walked away. I have to be honest with you; I had thought for sure this man was going to help me get home and yet all he said was "I will pray for you." Then it hit me! I wasn't done in this town. Who else did the Lord want me to meet? I mean come on, that was an amazing thing! "God, You had a man held over in the same town for two days so we could bump into each other." I looked forward to what would happen next.

15

OF JESTERS AND VETS

~

It was now Sunday, July 30th. I had been gone for three weeks, and I wondered, "Why can't I go home?" I was about to get my answer.

I decided to call Pastor Dorie and tell her where I was and what had been going on for the past week and a half. She told me that she and Jeff, along with the church, had been praying for my family and me. I told her that the Lord hadn't let me call until now because if I had told Pastor Jeff, he would have come and rescued me from whatever challenges I had. She said, "You're right. He would have." I told her that I had been talking to Darryl almost every day and that I would call her back soon. She prayed for me over the phone and said goodbye. I looked around at the park and asked, "Now what Lord?" The Lord told me to drive around town and stop at the places he told me to. So I drove to the grocery store and parked and waited for a couple of hours. Then the Lord had me drive to a hardware store, wait, and then to another grocery store, and then a gas station, and back to the park. I got the idea that He wanted people to know I was there. It was now late afternoon and I stayed at the park until it got dark and then drove back to the big dirt lot with the big rig trucks. I got out some of the food I had bought before the festival and ate a peanut butter and jelly sandwich. The way I was parked, I could see all the trucks and cars that came off the freeway exit ramp and turned to come into this town. I watched as cars and trucks filled up at the gas station and got on the on-ramp of the freeway heading south. I prayed, "Lord, I really want to go, but if that's not your will, I will stay another day."

Now, every town has a pawnshop of some sort and there were many times when I thought, "That's it, I'll pawn my DJ gear or my sound system. After all, I'm traveling with over twenty-five thousand dollars in gear. I know I can pawn this equipment and get home and start over." These thoughts, however, were not the Lord's thoughts, nor His plan. I had to trust Him.

I put up the sunshade in my front windshield and used two towels rolled up in my windows to give me some privacy as I tried to sleep. The big rig trucks came and went all night, and with them parked only a few feet away from me on both sides, I never really got any rest. By about 5:30 A.M., I had had enough. I just got out of the van and walked around for a few hours. I walked down to the park I was at the day before. I had some change, so I bought a cup of coffee at a little coffee hut across from the park and then walked back to my van. My low fuel light was on, but the Lord told me to drive around the town and through the outer areas as well. I looked at the odometer in my van and knew I could only drive twenty more miles and then I would be walking. I spent the whole morning driving to one part of town and then another, always stopping and waiting until the Lord told me to go again. I drove back to the park and made another peanut butter and jelly sandwich for lunch. I watched as another man walked through and came toward me. I was sitting at one of the picnic tables just off the sidewalk. As he got closer, I could hear him talking to himself and then he stopped at a tree and started yelling at it in a totally different voice. As if that wasn't interesting enough, he was wearing a court jester's hat with multiple bright colors and sequins, a shiny gold woman's blouse, blue jeans and tennis shoes. I thought, "Lord, do you want me to pray for him to be set free?" I didn't get an answer. As he continued walking through the park, he would stop every so often and yell at a trashcan or another tree. Cars drove by and honked and he would wave at them, make some strange noises and just keep going, until he was gone.

It was Monday, July 31st. I kept thinking, "How long is the Lord going to keep me here?" I could get a call at any moment from someone saying, "The Lord spoke to me Bobby, and I sent money to get you home." I guessed I wasn't to have an encounter with this man. So, I waited in the park for three hours until the Lord told me to go back to the dirt lot where I had spent the night. There were no more big trucks and no one else around anywhere. "What am I doing here?" I thought.

I parked the van and trailer and sat there for an hour. I looked in my driver's side mirror and saw something behind me, at the very outer edge of the dirt lot. I noticed a small storage building about as wide as a 2-car garage with a metal platform about two feet high and two wood storage units on top of it. I saw all this dust coming out from under the platform and then out crawled a man dressed in old army fatigues with two large shepherd dogs. I couldn't believe it. How did they get under there? As I started to walk towards them both dogs came charging at me. I was more than happy when the ropes around their collars pulled them back. The man motioned at the dogs and they stopped, both just sitting there. He came over to my van and trailer. I asked, "Are you okay?" He said, "Yes." I could see he had been on the road awhile. I asked him, "How long have you and your dogs been under that platform?" He answered that they'd been there since very early that morning. A truck driver had dropped them off. I said, "Are you and your dogs hungry?" Again, he said yes. The Lord said, "Give him all you have except your instant oatmeal." I told him, "I have peanut butter, jelly, canned food and soup that you just have to pop the top off of and eat." I also had some apples, water and some brand new socks. He looked at me in disbelief. He asked, "Why would you do this for me?" I told him how God was keeping me in this town and wouldn't let me leave yet. "So, I must still be here for you." There were big tears in his eyes. He told me he was a Vietnam vet and was on his way to Idaho. He said the two dogs had been with him for years and were the only friends he had. I asked him if he knew Jesus Christ as his Lord and Savior and he told me that yes, he did and that he had a Bible in his duffle bag. I asked, "Can I pray for you?" He said, "Please do." I prayed for him as he cried. When I was done I gave him all the water he could carry as well as the food. He thanked me again and said, "You don't know what this means to me, especially the socks." I said, "Yes, I do. I know on the road and on the streets, socks are better than gold." He smiled and said, "You are right."

Well, that had to be it, right? That was why I was still in this town. Now, for sure, God would make a way for me to leave. I felt so sure that I was finally finished there. Or was I? I sat in the van for a while and then I saw the man I had seen earlier in the park walk by. He still had his court jester hat on and was singing something. He walked past the dirt lot to the gas station and then I lost sight of him. I guessed I was still not meant to have a conversation with him. In any case, I didn't have any more gas, so now I would have to walk. The Lord told me, "Go back to the park." So, I did just that. It was about a mile and a half away. I really enjoy walking most of the time, but this was getting old. What I really wanted was to get on my way even if it was just over the hill.

16

COLD OATMEAL

~

When I got to the park I noticed about five teenagers sitting on a bench in the middle of the grass area. They were sitting there laughing and smoking cigarettes, and I thought, "Wait a minute, that isn't cigarette smoke." I could smell marijuana as I got closer. They stopped laughing and looked over in my direction. I just kept walking and sat down at a bench at the end of the park. As I watched them go back to laughing and smoking pot, I noticed one teenager at every corner of the park. I thought, "Something's up." One by one, the teenagers in the center of the park walked out to where the others were and took their place while the ones that had been at the four corners of the park came back to the center to smoke. Wow, what a great plan these kids had. They could see the police no matter which direction they might come from and they could warn their friends before the police would be able catch them. I thought, "Lord, You have to reach these young people some how, some way. Send people to tell them about you. If it's not me, Lord, send someone." The Lord told me He wanted to show me how sharp these kids were. He said that He wanted to use them for His kingdom because when they did come to know Him, they would be able reach others that would try to run and hide. But there is no place you can hide from His Love.

I thought about the two men I had met over the past two days by God's Divine Timeline while I walked back to the van. I was hungry, so I pulled out a bottle of water and some instant oatmeal and a plastic spoon. I poured the oatmeal into a cup and added water. So, cold oatmeal it was. I just sat at the end of my van and ate and watched as trucks and cars pulled into the dirt lot and the motel on the other side. There was a restaurant connected to the motel. I watched as people went into the restaurant and thought, "Man, it would be great to eat in the restaurant and have a motel room with a hot shower and a soft bed. I've been sleeping sitting up in my van and my back and neck are killing me. Well, it's been a day or two, I better call home." I called my wife and told her I was still in Baker City, Oregon. I had called her when I first got into town. She asked, "When are you coming back to Arizona and why are you not on the road?" "Well," I said, "I'm waiting on the Lord." She said, "You are waiting on the Lord? You are just sitting in that town waiting for God to tell you what to do?" I replied, "Yes." My wife said, "I just don't understand you." I couldn't tell her that I didn't have a dime and was eating cold oatmeal out of a Styrofoam cup.

I called Darryl and told him what was up. I knew no one was allowed to help me yet. I thought, "Tomorrow I will be able to leave." Darryl said he was praying and would talk to me soon. I got ready to try and sleep, but the noise of trucks and cars kept me awake all night. I was in pain and exhausted. Although I had been cleaning up the best I could at the gas station's bathroom and changing my clothes everyday, I hadn't had a shower in days. I had a huge bag of dirty clothes now. I couldn't sleep so I got out of the van at 4:30 A.M. on Thursday. Just then some truckers came out of their trucks, said hello to me, and walked over to get some coffee at the gas station. They came back and asked me what Not Of This World Productions was all about. I told them of the ministry God had given me and that I was on a journey. I also shared with them the stories of the two men I had met in this town over the past two days. They said, "You should write a book about the journey you are on. All the truck stops would carry it." Great idea, if I survived the journey. They said good luck and got back into their truck and took off. I watched as they pulled out of town. "Ok, God, now what?" I was still hungry so I ate some more cold oatmeal. As I was eating, I was thinking of the pictures we see of children in Africa and around the world who are starving and how they would give anything to have a cup of cold oatmeal. So I finished eating and walked back to the park.

17

WALK BACK TO THE PARK

~

There was a river that ran through the park. It also had a walking path and bike path. I saw a few people out for a morning walk, so I decided to see how far the trail went. It was a beautiful track along the water's edge that went on for a few miles. I walked a couple of miles and sat down on a tree stump and prayed. "God, is there someone you want me to help, someone who needs prayer in this town? Lord, my wife, children, family and friends think I have abandoned my family. I know that I have made mistakes, but whatever You want me to do, I will do it. Just lead me and I will follow the best that I can." I went back to the park and stayed there until about 1:30 P.M. Then I walked back to my van and ate some more oatmeal in a cup. McDonalds's was about forty yards away and man was I hungry for a hamburger! I was honestly praying for a hamburger! After a while, around 3:30 P.M., was when the Lord said, "Walk back to the park! Walk back to the park!" My response was, "I have been going to the park for days and there is no one there. Why do I need to go to the park? I'm tired of walking." Again, the Lord commanded me to, "Walk back to the park!" I knew that I should do as He said.

As I approached the park, there were a couple of trucks and some people who had just arrived and were pulling out sound equipment. I couldn't believe it. This place had been empty two hours ago and now there were people arriving with all kinds of supplies, a big grill, and ice chests full of something. They hung up a banner from one of the grocery stores that was apparently sponsoring them. I walked over and asked, "What's going on here?"   They said that they were having a free picnic for the public. It was drug awareness night and all across America they were having block parties and inviting the public to attend. The lady that was setting up food said they'd be ready around 5:00 P.M.   This was amazing. I was going to be first in line for a hamburger, that's for sure! I turned back to the people and asked if they needed any help. One of the men asked if I could help him with some speakers and an amp case. I was really excited. Finally, I was going to eat more than just oatmeal! They were going to have music and they told me the Fire Department, Police Department and the Mayor would be there as well as many other people from the community.

After I moved the sound equipment, I sat and watched them set up. I was thinking maybe I would hear some good country and western music. I wasn't sure, but either way it seemed this was the break that I really needed today. I called Darryl and told him what was going on and that I thought maybe the Lord would send me on my way after this event was over. As the musicians were setting up and doing their sound check, I sat and listened to them. Wait a minute. They weren't singing country music.   They were singing praise and worship songs from church. WOW! This was getting good. I needed this. Thanks, Lord! After they finished, the Lord said, "Go and tell the lead singer about you being here in Baker City." I said, "Lord, I haven't eaten yet and besides, they are going to think I'm crazy." Just about that time, the man with the court jester hat walked by. "Ok Lord, I'll tell him."

I walked over to the singer and said, "Could I talk to you for a minute?" He said sure and we walked over to one of the benches. I said, "My name is Bobby Dendy and I'm from Phoenix, Arizona. God sent me to a Christian festival in Washington and now I'm trying to get back to Phoenix. I've been here for three days with no money and very little food and I have people praying for me. I have my van, trailer and twenty-five thousand dollars worth of sound equipment parked on the edge of town. The Lord has used me to help some people while I've been here, but He will not let me leave this town yet and I don't know why." I took a deep breath and waited for his response. The man looked at me and jumped like someone touching a hot electric wire. He looked at me again and said, "I will take you over to my pastor. We have a booth set up for tonight to tell about our prison ministry from the church." We went over to meet the pastor and I told him the same story. He told me about their church and what the Lord had called them to do in the community. He asked me, "What kind of music do you play?" I told him all types of Christian music for the youth, as well as DJ led worship. I told him, "A lot of people don't understand what that means. Instead of a band and worship team, I play worship music from CDs that the Lord leads me to play." The pastor looked at me and said, "You need to come by our church tomorrow night. Our worship team practices on Wednesdays." I was thinking, "This guy doesn't get it. I want to leave this town." I asked, "Where is your church?" He told me that it was on the outer part of town and gave me directions. I told him that I didn't have gas to get there. He looked at me and said, "You will!"

I didn't want to hear that, I wanted to go. I called Darryl and told him that the Lord wasn't going to let me leave yet, but that I was going to get a good meal soon and that I would talk to him tomorrow. As soon as the food was available, I got a hamburger, some fruit, and a nice piece of cake. Life was good again. That night there were a few thousand people in the park. The Mayor spoke of the dangers of drugs to the youth in their community and the need to use everything they could to help youth and families affected by drugs. I stayed until everyone left and helped the worship team load their equipment back into the truck. The man I first talked to said, "Pastor says you are going to join us tomorrow for praise and worship." I told him, "If God makes a way." It was about 9:00 P.M. as I walked back to my van. "Looks like I'm here for another day."

18

WHO AM I KIDDING

~

The night was like all the others with trucks coming and going, sleeping only an hour or two from exhaustion and then waking up to the sound of truck noises. I was up early again and ate my oatmeal in a cup. I was thinking, "I have been here in this town for four days; maybe, just maybe, this is the day." I walked to the park and prayed.

It was about midmorning when I got a text from Darryl on my phone. Actually, it wasn't a text, but a photo of some guy with his head shaved. I looked closer and thought, "Why did Darryl send me a picture of some guy? Wait, is that Darryl?" I called him and said, "Darryl is that you with the shaved head?" He said, "Yes." I asked him, "Why did you do that?" He told me that he had been praying and fasting for me and my family and had asked the Lord if he could send me money to bring me home and the Lord had said, "No". He continued to explain that the Lord had told him to fast and shave his head. I just stood in the park with tears running down my face. You see, my friend works at a very large corporate company and is surrounded by professional people. His appearance is always immaculate from head to toe, everything perfect and every hair in its place. I asked Darryl, "What did they say to you at work today?" He replied, "They asked me why I shaved my head. I told them that I have a friend who is a missionary/evangelist and has been called to serve the youth of this country. He is stuck in a small town in Oregon and God won't let him out of that town. Yet, God won't let me send him money. So, the Lord told me to shave my head and pray for my friend." Darryl told me that he was glad that the Lord hadn't told him to rend his garments and put ashes on his head, but if God wanted him to do it, he would! I thought to myself that what Darryl had already done, to those who knew him, was just as if he had rent his garments and put ashes on his head. I pictured him that day as the people around him talked to each other about Darryl and why he had shaved his head. I thanked Darryl for being obedient to the Lord and for being my friend. He told me he would continue to fast until the Lord let me out of that town.

I walked back to my van still in shock over what my friend had done. I got into my van and sat there. I remembered I had thrown all my change into one of my small duffle bags and thought that maybe I could scrape together enough to buy a dollar hamburger at the fast food place. I dug around, gathered some coins and put them in my pocket. I was still looking for more change when I heard what I thought was someone playing a trumpet. I had my van door closed but I could still hear the trumpet music loud and clear. I got out and stepped around my trailer to see where the music was coming from. There on the corner, next to the hamburger joint, was an African-American man playing a trumpet and two teens on their mountain bikes watching him play. The whole picture didn't quite fit. I knew God was up to something again.

I walked over to the restaurant and bought a double cheeseburger from the dollar menu and had 83¢ left over. As I walked out, I could hear the man with the trumpet playing again. The Lord told me to go over and talk to him, so I did. He was dressed all in black, with a leather jacket over one arm and an old black music case at his feet. I told him that I really enjoyed the way he played. He said thanks. I asked him, "Where are you from?" He said he had been playing up in Seattle, Washington and that he had gotten a ride this far. He thought that he might go back to New Orleans or St. Louis; he wasn't sure. He said, "I have been talking to these two young men and they tell me that there is quite a problem with drugs in this town. I asked the boys what kind of drugs, and they told me marijuana. I asked them if they had lived here their whole lives and they said no. They moved here a year ago from Bakersfield, California to get away from the drugs there." He continued on, "We need to do something about this problem. We should work together to help." I replied, "I have been in this town for four days and I have seen with my own eyes that there is a drug problem here with the youth." Then I asked him, "Are you hungry?" He said no and that he was okay. The two boys said goodbye and took off on their bikes. I asked him again if he was hungry, and he said no. I had the eighty-three cents in my pocket so I told him, "I have to give this to you. It's all I have." He looked me in the eye and said, "I can't take all you have." I explained, "You have to. The Lord can't give me what I need next until I give Him all that I have left." He said, "Ok, I will take your eighty-three cents as the Lord instructs." I thanked him and started to head for my van. Before I left, I turned around and asked, "Where will you go next?" He responded, "Where do you live?" I answered, "Phoenix, Arizona." He said, "Maybe I'll see you sometime in Phoenix." I smiled and continued to walk toward my van when a thought occurred to me. He didn't have a duffel bag or a suitcase, just his trumpet case. I turned around to look again but he was no longer there. Where had he gone? Oh well, I thought, time to eat my hamburger and rest a bit.

Around 2:00 P.M. I called up my sister-in-law, Robin, and told her the latest. When I had finished, she told me she would wire me some money. She didn't say how much, but it didn't matter to me. I told her there was a grocery store that had a place to wire money. She said she would call me back and let me know when she had sent it. I can't begin to tell you how excited I was to leave. I wanted to get back home and tell my family what God had been doing through this journey. It was obvious He wanted me to reach these people. I mean, when I told my family the things that had happened and how God had arranged it, things would be better, right? I thought, Robin will probably send me at least a couple hundred dollars and with that, I might make it. She called me a little later and told me she had wired the money. I said, "Thank you so much." I went into the store, filled out the form and gave it to the lady behind the counter. She looked it over and said, "Everything looks fine, but you didn't fill in the amount sent. We have to have that information from you or we can't give you the money." So, I called Robin back. She told me that she had sent me fifty dollars. I told her thanks again but I could feel my heart sink. I knew that God was in control of what was happening and that I would have to surrender to it or else I would be stepping outside of His will and doing my own thing, which I knew wasn't the answer. So, I got the fifty dollars, put forty dollars in gas in the tank and started toward the on-ramp of the freeway. Suddenly, I pulled over to the side of the road. I knew I was supposed to go to the praise and worship practice at the pastor's church, but I had gas now and I just wanted to go. Man, who was I kidding? I found the piece of paper with the directions to his church, turned around and headed to the road just outside of town.

19

HARD BUT HONEST

~

I found the church. There were a few people already there. I said hello to the man and his wife from the park event. The wife said, "We knew you would make it." I told them, "The Lord won't let me leave yet." They said that the others would arrive in a few minutes. Remembering what I had told them the day before, they asked me, "Bobby, how do you worship as a DJ?" I explained, "I play songs from different CDs as the Lord leads me. I pray and the Lord tells me what to play." They asked, "Can you play tonight?" Well, my equipment was in the trailer and I could get it all out, but for some reason I was feeling really sick. I asked the Lord what He wanted me to do and He told me to play a CD that I had recorded while in a church in Tulare, California that had been having a revival. I asked them, "Do you have a CD player?" They told me there was one right under the mixing board. I explained to them that I always recorded what I was doing. It was all about the anointing of God. I said, "This CD has been used by God to touch a lot of people and He gets all the Glory." I set everything up and I asked them to let me know when the time was right, and I would play the CD. I said that it was over sixty minutes, mixed with no breaks between the songs.

When the rest of the worship team arrived, they began with their worship practice. They were very good and I could feel the presence of the Lord getting stronger. Then the worship leader introduced me to everyone and told me to start playing the CD. Everyone started to sing and worship along with the music. The presence of the Lord was really strong; some of the team got on their faces before the altar while the rest walked around the church and prayed. At the end of the CD, I got on the microphone and prayed for the church and then I went up to the altar and prayed for people individually. It was great to be able to bless them. Before I left, one of the couples came up to me and handed me twenty dollars. They said, "I know it's not much, but I hope it helps you." I told them it was perfect. They said, "Bobby, you should come by tomorrow morning. Our pastor meets once a month with other pastors from different churches here in town and you should tell them what the Lord has had you do while you have been here. It's important that the prophet speaks." I told them that I didn't think I would be able to. I was looking forward to getting on the road as soon as possible. I thanked them, left some worship CDs and headed back through town to the freeway. As I got closer, the Lord told me to stay one more night. I couldn't believe it. I felt sick, I was tired and the Lord was asking me to sleep sitting up in my van one more night. "Okay, Lord, I will do it. I will go to the meeting with these pastors if that's what you want." In spite of everything, I was also curious as to why the Lord would have me go to the pastor's meeting. So, here was to another long night in the van.

The next morning, I was feeling a little better. When I got to the church, I noticed another brand new church across the street. It was very nicely done with a new parking lot. The whole property was immaculate while the church I was at was in need of a new parking lot of its own as well as some other help. As I got out of the van and started walking around and praying for this church, the Lord showed me, in a vision, the new buildings that would be built on the property, down to their very size, shape and color. I prayed, "Thank you, Lord, for this pastor and this church." The Lord said, "They have made this property Holy Ground for My presence and I am going to bless them for it."

When I went inside the church, I found five pastors sitting at a table. The pastor of the church introduced me to the rest and explained to them, "This is Bobby Dendy. He has been in our town for five days and the Lord will not let him leave our town until he accomplishes what the Lord has for him to do. I believe he has a word from the Lord for us this morning." I said, "Thank you for letting me be here this morning. Let's pray before I tell you what is on my heart." So I prayed with the pastors and then I told them, "It needs to quit being about you and your ministry. It needs to be what the Lord wants." I continued on, telling the pastors about the events of the past four days and I told the pastor of the church that was hosting this meeting about the vision the Lord had shown me about his church and the new buildings. As I was speaking to him about the different buildings that would be on that property, one of the other pastors slapped him on the knee and smiled, saying, "See!" I knew as I was speaking that it was confirmation to the pastor and the others. I also asked them about the man in the park with the court jester's hat that I had seen walking all over town. They told me his name and explained that he had been like that for years. I looked at them and asked, "Why haven't any of you prayed for him to be set free?" There wasn't an answer, just a long pause. I continued, "Why doesn't anybody go out to the RV and trailer parks to minister to the elderly and those in the parks?" I had spent hours at one trailer park watching people just sitting outside their homes as their lives went by. I said, "Do any of you go to the trailer and RV parks to minister to the people and families?" Right then, the pastor sitting next to me broke down in tears. He explained that he hadn't had a church to pastor at for the past few years, so he had been doing prison ministry and helping others. The Lord had spoken to him a few months before about starting a ministry to those in RV and trailer parks. He went on to say that just a few days ago he and his family had been heading to a town north of Baker City to trade in the family car so that they could get an RV to do ministry in. As they were driving, a deer had run out in front of them and he hadn't been able to avoid it as it crashed into their car. They went off the road and their car was totaled. The family had received some bumps and bruises, but they were okay. He said that they now had no car and no way to get an RV for ministry. I looked around the table and told all the pastors there that they should help buy this man an RV so that he could do ministry with his family. I went on to tell the pastors that I had been in large churches of over five thousand people and small churches of less than sixty and denominations of all types. It had always amazed me that the gifts and talents that are in one church were always different from those found in other churches, large or small, and that if these churches would come together, we could accomplish so much more to show the Love of God to people and to lead them to know Christ. Due to denominational walls, we have done little to nothing to change this. I said, "I appreciate all of you for coming together to help each other. I believe God is directing this in the hearts of His servants. It is one thing to come together within the confines of the four walls of the church. It is quite another to take it outside the four walls to a culture that doesn't find the church or its people relevant for today. This is rapidly changing." I told them that unless God builds the House, they that build the House build it in vain.

We have to stop building 'our' house and ask the Lord how we should build 'His' house. There are so many books out about how to bring growth to a church and community, but if these books were the answer, we wouldn't be able to build churches fast enough.

By that time, all of the pastors were staring at me like I had just punched them in the nose. "You know," I told them, "You can't kill a dead man. For me, the past three weeks have been a non-stop dying to what I want to do and a birthing of the Lord's plan for my family and me. It has come through extreme pain and many tears for my whole family. It has become very evident that I have not been sent on a vacation by the Lord, but on an assignment to do His Will." I began to tell them another story.

About six years before, my middle daughter, Keeley (then four years old), asked me an interesting question while I was driving with her in the car. She was sitting in the back seat and said, "Dad, do you want to know the meaning of life?" I looked in my rear view mirror at her smiling face and I could see a glow around her. I thought of all the books in history that have been written to explain why we are here and what the purpose is for our life here on earth and then I answered her, "Yes, Keeley, I want to know the meaning of life." She answered me, "All we have to do is love God and help people." She said, "That is all we have to do Dad." I looked at her shining face and asked, "Who told you that, Keeley?" She smiled again and said, "Jesus." I asked, "When did He tell you that?" She replied, "Right now, Dad."

WOW! What if we did that? What if first, we loved God with our whole heart, mind, and soul and then, loved others with the Love of Christ? What would happen? I thought, "That's what Jesus did."

The pastors all looked at me and smiled. I said, "I believe the Lord is sending me across America to build relationships with those who have a burden for the youth of this country and for the lost, but I believe He will need to heal His children first. There are so many of us who are wounded because of the church and because of other

Christians and we desperately need to be healed. I have met wounded Christians all over the country." I told the pastors, "If God doesn't send revival by His Spirit, and not by the plans of man, it is over. Our country and culture has slipped so far away from God. Many people want to blame the youth of our country, but in reality, it is our fault. We have been so self-centered, wanting to get ahead in life, that we have left our children behind to fend for themselves and have let today's media raise our children and direct the moral path of our country." I shared that, "I asked my mom, who has been a Christian for over thirty years, a question recently. I said, 'Mom, in all your years in the church, have you ever seen or heard anybody stand up in front of the congregation and proclaim that they were called as a Missionary/Evangelist to our own country? That God had called them to reach the youth of this country?' My mom answered, 'No!' You know, we send young people as missionaries around the world but have done very little to encourage them to reach their own culture and their peers in this country." I told the pastors, "Don't get me wrong, I'm not saying that there are no ministries that are reaching out to the youth of this country, it's just not a priority for the majority of churches today in America." I told them that if they really wanted to know where we stood on reaching the youth of today that they should get Ron Luce's book "Battle Cry for a Generation." I told the pastors that this man and the ministry God had placed in him were exactly what we needed to do as a church, a family, and a country. I have read his books and watched the TV programs that he has for youth and he is right on target, but the challenge that I see him face year after year is that the church, American Christians, are not responding to the call of alarm. They act as though it's the underpaid, overworked youth pastor's job.

I looked at the pastors and said, "It is our job, and personally, I know I haven't done a very good one. How about you, gentlemen? If the fathers would turn their hearts toward their children, then the rebellious children would turn their hearts back to their fathers." I told the pastors that God had sent me on a road of brokenness and tears to get this into my spirit. I felt that God had given me a message to the body of Christ and if in that body I reached just one person, then that was my assignment. I thanked them for their time and I told them, "This may have been a hard word, but we are in a very challenging time that requires action from those of us who profess to be Christians." The pastor of the church asked me, "Bobby, what is it that you believe the

Lord would have you do to reach this generation?" I answered, "My wife, Cheryl had a vision a few years ago of us traveling across the country in large RVs and many big rig trucks like what you would see in major concert productions. She said people were calling us from cities all over the country asking us if we could come to their city. I believe we are to bring the biggest and most creative multimedia worship experience ever seen into those cities with the purpose of lifting up the Name of Jesus and that the Lord will touch, heal and draw those who do not know Him. Without the presence of God, it would just become an entertainment event and that is not what He has called me to do." I continued, "If we would come together and worship the Lord and repent, then the Lord would send the revival that this country so desperately needs and the Lord would draw the lost back into the church of America. Personally, I believe the youth of today are the 'last generation' talked about in the Bible and even if they are not, we should be acting as though they were." The pastors looked at me and agreed. I said, "There are millions of brokenhearted teens who need to be healed. In America today there are over thirty three million teenagers and more than half come from divorced and broken homes." I told the pastors that I believed that God was going to heal the men and fathers in this country so that we could become what the Lord intended us to be.

They asked if they could pray for my family and me. As they prayed, I knew that I was among brothers in the Lord that faced all the same issues that I did. It was great to have men come together to pray for each other. They asked, "Bobby, will you ever bring that type of experience to our town?" I told them that I believed that God would make a way for me to come back. I also told them that the Lord had told me that I would be in stadiums of thousands one night and a town of only hundreds the next; it was all about reaching those that He directed me to reach. As I said goodbye, I thought "I'll be back to this community sometime soon."

20

LISTEN, DO YOU HEAR THAT?

~

As I left Baker City that morning, I figured that with the gas and money I had, I could make it to Boise, Idaho where I had a brother and sister. I would finally be able take a shower and sleep in a real bed for at least one night. As I got closer to Boise, about thirty miles away, I called my sister and told her that I would be coming by to stay for a day or two if that was okay. My sister told me that she had talked to my mom and that she could not believe what I was doing to my family, or to my other brothers and sister, and that my abandoning my family was bringing up memories of what our father had done to us. She let me know that she did not appreciate it, that I was not welcome in her home and to keep driving. I tried to say something to her, but she just hung up the phone.

As I approached Boise, I cried. I just kept going down the freeway. I looked at my gas gauge; again, I wasn't going to make it far. The words came back to me again, "Keep going, there will be plenty of time to cry." I made it to Mountain Home, Idaho, pulled off the freeway and drove around a bit. "Oh well," I thought, "I wonder where the town square is or maybe the park." It didn't take long to find it. There, mounted on a cement column, was a military jet right at the entrance of the park. The thought came to me, "I wonder if this is a military town?" I parked my van beside the park just like I had in Baker City. The park was bordered by homes on two sides. I got out of the van and saw that there were just a few kids playing on the playground. It was about noon on August 4th. I stayed there for a few hours and then drove around town. I found out that there was a military base in Mountain Home. It was an Air Force base, which explained the Air Force jet in the park. I stopped the van and called my sister-in-law Robin who lived in Denver, Colorado. I told her what my sister in Boise had said to me and that I was now in another small town in Idaho. She said, "You might as well find a church." "A church?" I asked. "What church, Robin? I want to get on the road. I don't want to sit in this town for days. I need to go right now." As I was talking to her on the phone, I looked across the street at the small businesses in the town. I saw a pawnshop, and for a brief moment the thought flashed across my mind, "I'm going to pawn my equipment and get out of here!" Robin interrupted my thoughts with, "Bobby, did you hear me?" I said, "Yes, but I haven't seen any churches yet, just the park and some small stores." She said, "You will need to find a church." I said, "OK!"

After I hung up the phone, I drove back to the park. There wasn't a single person there. I looked toward the far end of the park and saw what looked like a stage. Well, that was strange. I hadn't seen it earlier. So, I walked over to the stage. It was built on a twenty-four foot trailer bed that could be pulled by a truck. It was designed well. I was thinking, "Why is this mobile stage just sitting here in this park?" Just then a large truck pulling a custom concession trailer pulled right into the middle of the grass. My mind was racing, "Oh boy, here we go again!" I walked over to the truck and was greeted by a man and his wife. I asked them why they were parked here and they told me that there was going to be a concert in the park that night and they were contracted to do the food for the event. They asked me if I was from the area and I replied that no, I wasn't and proceeded to share with them the story of the journey God had me on. "Well, God will make a way," they said. They were both Christians and they told me about how God had brought them together. Afterwards, they said, "I hope you are hungry. When we get set up, come back and we will give you whatever you like." They went back to getting ready and a few minutes later another truck pulled through the park with an enclosed trailer behind it. Two men got out and started to set up sound equipment. I didn't bother them as they clearly had their set up plan together. I figured I would get a chance to talk to them later.

Two more cars pulled up along the park, just behind my van and trailer. A family of four got out of one car and stood next to my trailer reading the poem *Happytown*. It is always interesting to watch people who read the poem and the expressions on their faces when they are done. I got an e-mail one time from a man who said that he read *Happytown* while he was on his motorcycle following behind me at a traffic light. He told me how it had ministered to him that day and that he had gotten my e-mail address from my website that was on the trailer. The families that had just arrived made their way over to the stage and started to talk to the soundmen. After they were done, I walked up to one of the men and introduced myself and asked what was going to happen that night. He told me that they were a swing-jazz band consisting of nine men and that they were playing a concert in the park; an event that was booked through the city. The man asked me, "Is that your van and trailer?" I told him that it was. He said that he and his wife had enjoyed the poem. He asked, "What are you doing here in Mountain Home?" I told him a little about my journey and how I had gotten this far. He told me that all the guys in the band were Christians and that they had met at a Christian college in Oregon. In college, they had formed a band and worship team. A couple of the guys were now youth pastors at their churches. He also explained that they had a talent agency that booked them for these types of events and it was a lot of fun when they got to come together to play swing, jazz and big band music. They had crazy costumes and skits that they performed during the two-hour show. He told me he hoped I would really enjoy it. I told him that I was looking forward to it and then he went off to do a sound check as other members of the group arrived and started setting up.

It wasn't long before the park was filled with people. The line at the concession trailer was pretty long, so I decided to wait. The band was very good and they had the people in the park laughing and dancing along with the music. Throughout the show it was easy to see all the fun that the band members were having with each other on stage. After they finished their last song, there was a whirlwind of activity as everyone packed up to leave. My new friends from the concession trailer came over to the bench that I was sitting on and said, "We were looking everywhere for you." I told them that the line had been long and that I hadn't wanted to bother them. They apologized as they explained that they had sold out of food and had nothing left to give me. They said that had never happened before. I told them it was okay and that I was happy that they had made some money for all their hard work. The wife then told me that she had made some hard-boiled eggs that morning and, if I liked, she would bring them over. I wasn't in the mood for eggs at the moment, but then I remembered what the Lord had told me, "Eat whatever is put before you." So I accepted her offer. After bringing me the eggs she said, "God bless you, Bobby," then they got into their truck and left.

I was sitting by myself in the park with the wind whipping through these huge trees all around when a man walked over and asked, "Are you alright?" I looked at him and said, "Listen, do you hear that?" He said, "Hear what?" I told him, "The wind through the trees. It's so beautiful." He sat on the bench with me for a few minutes and said, "You are right." He quietly got up and left as I finished my boiled eggs.

21

FIELDS OF FLOWERS

~

What was I going to tell my wife now? I was sure my sister has already told her of our phone conversation that morning and I was emotionally and physically exhausted. I couldn't take another phone call, so I decided I would try and get some sleep. It had been five days of sleeping in the van since the music festival in Washington. I drove back out to the freeway. It was away from town and dark, so I thought I would be able to sleep out there. There was one gas station at the freeway entrance, so I used the restroom and then parked my van in a dirt lot just outside the reach of the lights. I got everything ready just like all the other nights in Baker City, but this time there were no big rig trucks to wake me up. I was excited about that. I finally closed my eyes for about an hour when I heard and felt a rumbling sound. It got louder and louder and the van was shaking. Then suddenly I heard a loud train horn that scared me to death. I couldn't believe it. I was parked about forty yards away from the tracks, and by morning's first light three more trains had passed through.

I drove back into town that morning and headed to the park. I walked across the street to get a cup of coffee and then I sat under a tree on a park bench for a couple of hours. I thought, "Ok, Lord, now what?" Then I remembered my sister-in-law's word from yesterday, "Find the church". Oh, great. I didn't have any gas so I would have to walk around town until I found a church. "You know, God," I said, "Couldn't I just ask somebody to help me? Couldn't I ask someone to loan me the money to go home?" The answer came back, "NO!" Ok. I guess I was going to find the church. I walked to the other end of the park to use the restroom and when I came out I noticed what looked like a cross on the top of a building just a block down one of the streets. So I walked down the street and, sure enough, as I got closer, there was a church with a big cross on it. I went back to the park and got my van and drove to the church parking lot. I parked and then looked around for an open door to the church, but they were all closed. I knocked on the door but no one answered, so I decided to head back to my van. Then a side door opened and a man stepped out and asked, "Can I help you?" I told him, "I was told to find a church for help. I'm from Arizona and God has sent me on a journey and I'm trying to make it back to Phoenix." He said, "Come on in."

I locked up the van and followed him into his office. The door was open and sitting in one of the chairs across from his office desk was a young lady in her mid-twenties. He introduced her as his youth pastor. He said they had just been having a meeting on how to reach the youth of their town. He explained, "There is nothing for them to do, so drugs and teen pregnancy are a big problem." The youth pastor asked me about the ministry the Lord had given to me. I shared with her a little bit about my background and then she asked, "How did you get here?" I told her about the music festival in Washington. She said that the church had taken some youth last summer, but not this year. I told her about how God had been using me to touch people's lives through praise and worship. As the three of us were talking, the presence of the Lord came down. The pastor looked at me and started to tell me of the prophetic journey God had had me on and how it was similar to Saul's prophetic journey in the Bible. He began writing down and explaining the journey with all the Scripture references and what each word of the journey meant in Hebrew. It was amazing. And as He was speaking I was just crying.

I know, I know. You're thinking, will this guy ever stop crying? I confess, at times I cry even as I write this story to you.

When the pastor was done giving me the definitions of the names of Saul's prophetic journey and finished explaining how they related to me, his youth pastor also started crying and told me that the Lord had shown her a vision of me standing in Heaven among a huge field of flowers as far as the eye could see. The flowers were all different colors. She said, "Bobby, the Lord told me that each one of the flowers represented a soul that you have touched through your obedience to God and the Lord says, 'These flowers represent all of the seeds you've planted on earth to reach the lost.'" Then the Lord moved on me as I gave a prophetic word to her and to the pastor. It was a powerful time in the presence of the Lord. The pastor took out a checkbook and wrote me a check. He said it wasn't much, but he hoped it would help get me down the road. He said, " And I'm sure you are hungry and could use a shower." I told him, "That would be great." He called one of the ladies who is a part of their drug and alcohol ministry to see if she could pick up some food for me and bring it to the church. He asked, "Would a hamburger and fries do?" I smiled and answered that it would be fine. He said, "Bobby, you will like this lady and her husband. They head up our drug and alcohol ministry and they meet tonight at the church. You should come and share your testimony and the journey God has you on." He asked, "Could you stay for a few days?" I told him that I would love to, but that I had promised a pastor friend in Arizona that I would do worship at his youth camp in 3 days. I had to make it back to Arizona. I told him, "I believe the Lord will send me to your church and town again and next time I will bring the whole event with me."

He showed me to where they had a shower there in the church. He told me it hadn't been used in a couple of years and they had just had a meeting on remodeling this bathroom for this very reason; if someone needed a place to shower and sleep for the night. He said, "I'm sorry we didn't have time to straighten it up." I told him it was okay. I can't tell you how good it felt to take a long hot shower. When I was finished, the pastor had a hamburger, fries and coke waiting for me. He told me that he had to leave to pick up his wife from work and said, "I hope you make it to the meeting tonight. It starts in a couple of hours." I said I would try.

It was Friday, August 4th. I had looked at the check and it was for seventy-five dollars, enough to get on the road again. The meeting was two hours away. If I left now I could make it to a bank and be gone. Of course, you can probably guess by now what I did. I was waiting at the church when the first person got there. I introduced myself and told him that the pastor had asked me to attend his meeting tonight. The man told me I was welcome to join them. It was a night full of individual stories of God's Love and Mercy. They normally had a potluck and bible study but because of my being there, the pastor asked me to share my testimony instead. This night would be different. I asked them to share with me first what the Lord had done in their lives. When it was my turn, I got to share my testimony and about the journey that I was on, and that even though it was full of tears and trials, God was in the middle of it. Before I left, they took up a love offering to help me out. It was a little bit over $70. I thanked them for everything and left the church. Then I went to the gas station just around the corner and filled up. I wouldn't be able to cash the check that the pastor had given me until the next day, but now I had gas and I was on my way.

22

NOT THIS ONE, THAT ONE

~

It had been weeks since I had slept in a bed and I would be sleeping in the van again that night. I drove until I made it to the middle of Utah and then slept at a rest stop in the van. It was Saturday and I needed to be at the youth camp by Monday. I cashed the check from the pastor and put all of it into the gas tank except for about five dollars, which I put aside for food. I continued on through Utah, determined to make it to Cedar City. I was still concerned with the cracks in the frame of my trailer, as they were getting bigger. As I drove with my window down I could also hear what sounded like a rock or nail in one of my tires. When I finally pulled over at a rest stop to check it out, I couldn't find anything, so I decided to keep going.

I called my wife and told her that I was in Utah. She knew I was going to Pastor Greg's youth camp and asked what I was doing now. I told her that I had a few more stops before I got to Arizona. By now, I had been gone for almost a month and definitely had not won over my wife or family. I couldn't explain to them. Who would believe me anyway? My mom would call every once in a while but I couldn't answer her questions. It was just enough for me to make it to the next hour of the day. I was thinking as each day went by, "Lord, I don't feel like I'm getting any closer to bringing healing to my marriage and my family." But, as I said earlier, you can't kill a dead man and I was pretty much dead to my will and open to what the Lord wanted me to do. It was now obvious that I would drive when He wanted me to, I would wait when He wanted me to and eat whatever was brought to me, even if that was nothing.

As I was driving, I realized that I would only make it as far as Beaver, Utah. I pulled off the freeway in Beaver, with the low fuel light on. As I drove around town, I thought, "Here I go again." It was much smaller then the other two towns that I had visited. I stopped at a small grocery store and asked if there was any place that had a way to receive wired money. He told me that no one in town had that ability and that the closest town where I would be able to wire money would be Cedar City. Oh Man! This was getting to be too much for me. I sure was tired of this. I thought, "I will just go back to the freeway, put five dollars and forty cents into the gas tank and if I get stuck on the side of the road, oh well." I drove back out of town toward the freeway and saw there were two gas stations to choose from. I thought, "What is my problem? Just pick one!" I drove over to one gas station, got out of my van and felt, "this is not the one." So I got back into my van and drove thirty yards to the other station.

There was only one attendant. He said the other guy had just got a call and had taken the tow truck to pick someone up. I asked him how far Cedar City was from here. When I heard how far it was, I just said, "Great. I'm not going to make it." The gas station attendant asked me how much I had to put into the tank. I answered, "five dollars and forty cents." He said, "Let's see how much I have in my pocket." He said, "I have four dollars and some change. Put ten in the tank." I went out and put ten dollars worth of gas in the van and then came back into the station. I told him, "Thanks, I only have two days to get to a youth camp in Payson, Arizona." He said, "Youth camp?" I said, "Yes, my friend is a pastor in Cottonwood, Arizona and runs two group homes for youth." The attendant then smiled and asked, "Is his name Greg Roeller?" I just looked at him for a moment and said, "Yes." He then told me that he had met Greg in high school. He had been a student in Cottonwood. He said that Greg was a teacher's aide and had invited him to one of his Bible studies and that was when he got saved! I was amazed! I told him, "I'm a DJ. I live in Phoenix and Greg invites me to Cottonwood to minister to the youth sometimes." I told him that one of the times I went there a young lady from the high school had given her testimony of how she had been saved by a poem she found taped to the wall in the high school. She shared about a boy she knew who had gotten saved at Greg's bible study and then pasted hundreds of

Happytown poems all over the school. When she read one of the poems, God had spoken to her through it and it changed her life. Now, she had come that night to read the poem. I told him, "I was there that night playing music." He looked at me with big eyes and said, "You are that DJ." He had also been there that night. I told him, "If you go out there to my trailer, you will find the *Happytown* poem written on three sides." He was excited and said, "When you see Greg, tell him a Cottonwood boy helped you get to camp." I told him I would and headed out to my van. Okay God, that was truly amazing!

23

GREET THEM BY NAME

~

I got on the freeway. I was about sixty miles from Cedar City and hundreds of miles away from my final destination; or so I thought. I made it to Cedar City and I called Darryl and my sister-in-law in Colorado. I told them that I was finally in a town where someone could wire me money, but the place was only open until 8:00 P.M. The time came and went and nothing happened for me. I got very frustrated and said, "I have had enough!" Across the street from the grocery store where I was parked, there was a bar. It was their grand opening and I planned to get out of here one way or another. I was thinking that I would walk over there and sell them some of my gear so I could get home. So, I walked into the bar. There weren't many people there. They had a stage all set up for a band and a few lights. I thought, "This should work out fine." I asked the bartender if the owner was in. She told me that he would not be in until the following night because he was on a road rally with some other bikers. I said, "Is the manager in?" She said that he wouldn't be in for a couple of hours. She asked, "Can I help you?" I said, "No, thanks." She asked, "Can I get you a drink?" Again, I said, "No, thanks. I gave that up sixteen years ago, but thanks for your time." *I get it God. I will drive around until you tell me to stop or I run out of gas.*

I drove all over town. Cedar City is predominantly a Mormon community with a large Mormon college. The whole area was beautiful, surrounded by red rock mountains. Once again, I was just about out of gas. I pulled up along a sidewalk in a residential neighborhood. I happened to pull up in front of a very unique looking two-story house or apartment. I wasn't sure, but I thought I could see a gas station about twenty-five yards away, so I got out and walked over. There was a station after all and I asked the man running it, "Is there any way you would let someone get gas here if they called it in to you on their credit card?" I told him that I was stuck and that the only place that I could get money wired to me was closed. He said it was against their policy but he would do it for me. I walked back to the van just as a man and his wife stepped out of the house I was parked in front of. As I was looking for my phone book so that I could call someone for help, the man and his wife stood on the sidewalk and read *Happytown*. When they were finished reading, I asked them whether this was a house or an apartment. They explained that it used to be two apartments but that they had converted it into one house. I told them it had a lot of character and looked like an artist's home or a musician's home. I thought it would be a great place to house a music studio for a musician. They both looked at each other and said, "It is!" They introduced themselves and the man told me his wife was a singer/songwriter and he was a musician. I told them that I was a designer/artist in stone. They asked, "Really?" I answered, "Yes, I have my portfolio with me if you want to see some of my work." They said, "We would love to." I mentioned, "I don't want to keep you from dinner." They told me that they had already eaten and were just on their nightly walk. They asked, "Would you like to come into our house and see the recording studio?" I told them I would love to. They opened the door and showed me around the two story, converted brick home. It had wood floors and was expertly decorated by an interior designer. I really enjoyed this home. I told them, "I have worked with some very high end designers and this is set up very well." They also showed me the recording studio upstairs. I told them that I was jealous. They laughed and asked me if I wanted a soda as we sat at their kitchen table to look through my portfolio. They asked me all kinds of questions about the different pieces of art and what kind of stone I used and about the homes and people I designed for. I answered their questions and told them, "I have a lot more projects that are not in my portfolio." They said, "It is very obvious that you have a lot of talent. Your work and designs are beautiful. Why aren't you doing your art full-time?" I told them that a few years before I had had a change of heart about the priority of my artwork over my ministry to young people. They said, "Would you like to go for a walk with us? We would like to hear how you got to Cedar City. We read your van and trailer. You are a Christian?" I said, "Yes, I am." Then I decided to ask them if they were Mormon. They said, "Yes. Would you like to go to a Christian coffee house? It's just around the corner. We know the owner and go there all the time." I said that I would love to.

As we were walking to the coffee house the husband said, "Bobby, you told us back at our house that the Lord has brought you into our town and that you only barely made it here. Now you don't have a dime and you are going to wait until the Lord makes a way for you to leave." I said, "Yes." "So, you have no money and God moves you and directs you as He pleases." Again, I said, "Yes." "But you still have choices?" "Yes, I can do it my way or I can do it as the Lord leads. If I had done it my way, I wouldn't have met you and your wife or the many other people I've encountered over the past four weeks." So, he asked, "Do you believe God has brought you here to meet us?" I came right back at him with the question, "What do you think?" Just then, we arrived at the coffee house and went inside. It was first class all the way. They introduced me to the owner and I looked around the little shop. It had a stage and was designed like a large living room with bookshelves, coffee tables and couches all around. It had a big screen along one wall and a sound booth with a computer. I thought, "Someone has done it the right way." As I was standing there taking in my surroundings, the husband was telling the owner how we had come to meet and that I was on a journey for God, a missionary if you will. I gave the owner my card and told him that I was a Christian DJ and that I played all types of Christian music. I explained how the Lord had really been directing me over the past few years to do DJ led worship. The owner just looked at me like, "Okay, whatever." I thought to myself, it's not like I haven't seen or experienced that look or attitude before. He then told me that they booked Christian bands for Fridays and Saturdays. The husband went on to tell the owner that I was in need of some help to get on with my journey and the owner just looked at me without saying a word. The husband asked me, "Would you like something to drink or eat? I will pay for it." The owner was standing right next to us. I looked in his direction and answered, "No, thanks, I'm fine." The husband looked at me and said, "Okay, let's go then."

As I walked down the sidewalk together with my two new friends, the husband said, "I don't get it. Why didn't he offer to help you? I said, "We all have chances to help people everyday and many times we simply choose to ignore it and don't look to see if we can help. Many times it's just smiling at someone and saying hello." Then I asked him, "Have you ever been in a store and noticed how people don't even acknowledge the person waiting on them or serving them? They wear a name tag with their name written right there and we don't even say their name." He asked me, "What do you do?" I said, "I call them by name, make eye contact, and ask how their day is going. You should see the shock on their faces that someone would even care." He looked at me and smiled.

As we left the coffee shop behind, the wife said, "The walk we usually take is a beautiful one along a lighted path and it takes about forty-five minutes to complete, will you be okay?" I told her that I would be okay. I asked them how long they had been married and where they had met. They told me they met in college. I asked if they were going to have children and they said some day. They asked about my family and how they were taking my being away. I told them that my family was not taking it very well, but that one day this would all make sense to them. Then they asked me, "How did you become a Christian?" I told them that my mother and my two brothers and two sisters were all Christians. I explained that I was the oldest of five and that my dad had been a drug addict and alcoholic and that I never got to know him. He would come in and out of our lives every few years, a few being five or six years or longer. I told them about how I had been a nightclub DJ and entertainer for fourteen years before I was saved and that my mom and family had been praying for me to come out of the darkness I was in. I said that I had known God was calling me, but I didn't want to answer. I thought that if I gave my life to Christ, it would be boring. Then the last two years of my life as a nightclub DJ were very bad. I was a hardcore alcoholic and drank every night. The nightclub owners didn't care as long as their cash registers were ringing and the dance floor was full. I was killing myself and there was no one to stop me.

The couple listened intently as I continued on, and I shared with them the story of my testimony.

24

TURNING POINT

~

I remember three times specifically when God sent people with a message for me. The first came one night as I was working at the club. Every Friday and Saturday, I would play music in the bar from 8:00 P.M. to 3:00 A.M. The place was packed and I was the life of the party. I was always buying people drinks on my tab as they came up to the DJ booth. One night a man approached the booth and said, "Hi." I asked him who he was. He didn't answer, he just smiled at me and said, "Bobby, God has a plan for your life and it is not in here. You will work with youth." I thought, "That's great." Then I turned to get a record and when I turned back, he was gone. But that was impossible! I was elevated in the DJ booth and could see all the way to the front door of the club. I never saw him again.

On Fridays and Saturdays, I never remembered driving home after 3:00 A.M. I would check my car when I woke up the next day, around 2:00 P.M., to see if I had hit something or somebody. It wasn't a very good life. I moved into a house with my fiancée and her daughter. I somehow arranged to not work on New Year's Eve in 1989. I was out at different clubs with my fiancée and it was 11:30 P.M. when she handed me a beer and said, "Do you want a shot or anything else?" To my surprise, I told her, "No!" I just didn't feel like drinking any alcohol, which was a first for me. I didn't drink the beer and I haven't had a drink since. It seemed God was working in my life in many different ways before I even knew how to recognize Him.

It was a few days later when two of my sisters came to my house at 3:30 A.M. I answered the door and my sisters said, "You need to come to the hospital quick." Chris, my younger brother, had shot himself in the head and they didn't think he would make it through the night.

*****

By now both of my new friends were totally quiet. I asked them, "Are you sure you want to hear all of this?" They said, "Yes" and we kept walking.

*****

When I arrived at the hospital they brought our family into this small room to brief us on what was happening. We were waiting for my other brother to arrive before they gave us the news, his supervisor was driving him from his job to the hospital, so I went outside to meet him and we walked into the hospital together. I led him to where the rest of the family was waiting. When we were all gathered, they told us it didn't look good. Chris had lost a lot of blood and the bullet had hit his skull and shattered into the back of his brain. I'm not sure I even comprehended all they were telling us, but I just remember my mom telling them that she had a promise from God that all of her sons would serve Him. She said, "My son will survive and come back to thank each and everyone that is working on him right now." When my mom spoke, it was with such authority and assurance, it just overrode what they were telling us was happening at the time. I thought to myself in that moment, what is it that my mother has that shatters the reality of the situation to pieces? I mean, what is it? Then it hit me. Her faith and the Lord's promise to my mom were her strength. The nurse said, "It just so happens that the best neurosurgeon at the neurological center was on call here and your son is in surgery at this very hour with him."

*****

As we continued to walk on the pathway, the man and his wife were wiping away tears from their eyes. I went on with the story.

*****

After they told us what was happening, I stepped out into the hall with my brother, Tim. I was so mad. I said, "Tim, where is this devil? I want to meet him now. I want to fight him. I want him to show himself to me right now!" My brother calmly said, "Bobby, you can't fight him in the natural. It's only through Jesus Christ that you will have the power to defeat him, not on you own." My brother Chris was a twin, and his twin sister Kate was very distraught. Chris had inherited a major chemical imbalance from all the drugs and alcohol my father had done. My brother and sister are fourteen years younger than me. I found out that some kids at school had threatened to beat my brother up and he had bought a gun out of the newspaper for sixty dollars. He was living at home with our mom and Kate. He had just broken up with his girlfriend and hadn't taken his medicine. He had been drinking and was obviously depressed and went for the gun he had hidden under his bed. It was there in his room that he used the gun.

My brother Tim had left me to check on the rest of the family. It was like a scene out of the movies. The sun was coming up and the light was shining through the blinds. I walked over to the window and watched the sunrise and then I told the Lord, "I know you have been knocking on the door of my heart for years and I haven't answered. So, I will make you a deal. If You save my brother I will serve You for the rest of my life and do what I can to stop other young people from trying to take their lives." It's funny how we think we can make the Creator of the Universe a deal, but it was all I had left. Well, over the next few days my brother had to go through another surgery. They had tried everything and the final thing was to put him into a medicated coma to bring down the swelling in his brain.

25

MY WAY

~

My mom and my family invited me to church. I thought there was just no way that I could possibly go. I mean, come on, I felt so dirty with the things I had done in my life. How could God use me? My brother was now in a coma and the weight of the situation was more than I could handle. My mom said, "Bobby, come to church with us tonight." So, I went to church that night for the first time in about eighteen years. When the usher greeted me at the door I could barely lift my eyes to say hello to him. I had been in darkness so long that I thought I knew what light was, but it wasn't God's light. I was in these clubs and I was deceived and no one had been able to lead me out of darkness. The Bible says that the devil comes as an angel of light. Well, the lights of that lifestyle had blinded me; the fast cars, gold, diamonds, money and fame at every level. All of the illusions were being unraveled in a moment by one servant at the door of the church; one servant who said hello and held out his hand.

The service started with praise and worship and everyone stood, except me. I couldn't. I kept thinking, I'm thirty-one years old and I threw away my life for chasing the things of the world. I was chasing something to make me feel like I was "somebody" but was just left empty. My brother had barely even started his life and now he was in intensive care in a coma. The service continued as the pastor got up and started his sermon. He had been preaching for only a few moments and then stopped and looked out into the congregation of over one thousand people. I was way in the back sitting with my family with my head down, but I heard him say, "Who is the one here tonight that has lived his life like the song 'My Way' and the Lord has brought you here now?" It was like time froze for a moment. I couldn't believe what I was hearing. He was talking to me. 'My Way' was my closing song in the nightclubs. It didn't fit the type of club music I played all night, but it was my anthem and everybody knew it, from the doorman to the bartenders. I mean everyone. Every Friday and Saturday night for years I had played Elvis' 'My Way', the same song that Frank Sinatra made famous. And when that song came on at 3:00 A.M., everyone knew the night was over. I used to tell the bartenders that when I died, I wanted *'he did it his way'* engraved on my tombstone. The song talks about how he did it his way, regrets he had a few, but he did it his way. Those lines in that song were what I lived by. I didn't have a father to show me or lead me, so I made my own rules and planned to live and die by them.

When the pastor asked, "Who are you here tonight that has lived like the song, 'My Way'?", I knew it was me. He continued, "God has brought you here tonight and the weight of the world is on your shoulders and you can't move anymore. God has called you and you are here tonight. Every head bowed and every eye closed, lift your eyes to meet mine. I would like to pray for you to receive Christ tonight. Where are you?" Slowly I lifted my eyes to meet the pastor's eyes and, as the Lord is my witness, an incredible white beam of light came from the top of that huge church and shown directly on me and the pastor led me in the sinner's prayer. That night I gave my life to Christ and immediately the weight was lifted off my shoulders. I turned to my brother Tim and said, "Tim, it was me." He looked at me and said, "We know. We've been praying for you for years."

In the next two weeks, the doctors were amazed at my brother Chris' progress. They told us that they had thought that he would never be able to walk or talk to us again. But they were wrong.

*****

I told my new friends that I had seen and experienced the power of God first hand and had dedicated the last sixteen years of my life to help youth around the country. They had already heard a few of the stories that had brought me to their doorstep and now they knew the drive behind this mission I was on. On the way back to their house we stopped at the gas station and the husband told me, "Go and bring your van over to the gas station, Bobby. Do you want a soda?" I told him that I would love one. Then I went and got my van and pulled into the gas station. He took out his credit card and said, "Let's fill it up." After the van was full of gas, he handed me $20 and said, "This is for a hamburger or something to eat." I told him and his wife, "Thank you so much." They said, "We hope to read the book about your journey someday." I laughed and said, "You will." They warned me that my route to Page, Arizona would be dangerous this late at night as there were a lot of deer out this time of year. I told them I would make it and headed out on the highway again.

26

IT WILL BE

~

I had a lot of ground to cover and it was already 11:00 P.M. I drove for about an hour and a half and then stopped out in the middle of nowhere. I grabbed a bottle of water and then got out of the van and poured it over my head to try and wake up. I looked up at the sky and the stars seemed like they were almost close enough to touch. I got back into the van and kept driving. I saw a few deer on my way. They came right up to the road and almost ran out in front of me, but God kept me safe. I finally made it to Page around 3:00 A.M. and found a department store parking lot where I stopped and tried to get some sleep. I couldn't fall asleep, however, because there were two very drunk men sitting on the parking lot curb, talking. I thought, "This is crazy." So I left the store and pulled into the lot of one of the only grocery stores in the area and tried to get some sleep. I was able to rest for about an hour and then the sun came up. I got out of the van and walked over to a fast food restaurant and got some breakfast. I decided to call Pastor Greg and tell him, "I'm stuck in Page, Arizona." Greg said he would see what he could do to wire me some money, but that it might take a few hours. I replied, "I'm not going anywhere." So, I took out a camp chair from my trailer and set it outside my van door. I had been sitting there for about an hour when a man came out of his motor home and began walking his dog just outside the parking lot edge. He came over to me with his dog and said, "Beautiful view, isn't it." I said yes it was. He said, "I like your trailer." I asked, "Did you read *Happytown*?" He said he did and that he liked it. He asked, "Where are you going?" I told him, "Eventually Payson, Arizona but I'm stuck here for now." He said, "Stuck?" I told him a little bit about the past few days of my journey that had gotten me here. He told me that he and his wife drove to Canada every summer, stayed there for a few months and then came back to Phoenix. I told him that I was from Phoenix. He asked about my ministry and where my family was. I told him that my family had stayed in Phoenix. He said, "Do you think they will ever be able to travel with you?" I told him, "That's my dream." "Well, that's my wife coming out of the store," he said, "I'd better go help her." And off he went with his dog.

I was thinking, "When is this going to end?" I sat there in my chair, almost falling asleep when I heard a loud horn. I looked up and saw the man I was talking to a few minutes ago motioning for me to come over to his motor home. I walked over and he introduced me to his wife. He said, "I wish I could help you more." He handed me a twenty-dollar bill. I told him, "Thank you so much." He said, "Don't give up, son. God has a plan for all this. Don't give up." I told him that I wouldn't. A little later I got a hold of Greg and he told me that he had wired me some money. He said, "I hope it's enough." I had learned enough by then that I just said, "It will be." Then I went and got the money and filled up at the gas station.

The brakes on the van were getting so bad that all you could hear was metal on metal. I decided to see if I could drop off the trailer in Cottonwood, Arizona where my friend and his family lived. It took me a few hours but I finally made it to Cottonwood. I had promised my wife that I would come and see my children before I went to the camp with Greg and the young people he was taking from the group homes he was running. My brakes were so bad that I wasn't even sure they could stop my van, even without the trailer, but I said a prayer and made it back home to Phoenix.

27

NO WELCOME

~

It had been one month since I was back home. My children were happy to see me but they still didn't understand why I had been gone for so long. My youngest daughter, Casidie, was very upset. She was only eight years old and also autistic. We really had never been away from each other for more than a day or two. My middle daughter, Keeley, was hurt and confused by the choices she thought I was making; my choosing not to stay in Phoenix, not to get a full-time job, and not to quit doing the ministry for youth. My oldest daughter, Kristyn, wanted nothing to do with me. I can't even tell you how much that crushed me. I love her so much. She was four years old when my wife and I got married. And now she was so mad at me. My wife thought that when she told me to leave a month ago that I would go out, get a full-time job and that we could work things out from there. Instead, it looked like I was on some summer Christian-vacation. She wanted me to leave and get an apartment on my own for a year and prove to her and my children that they would come first. So, I wasn't walking back into my home like a triumphant hero. No one cared about my stories and honestly no one, especially my wife, wanted to hear anything about them. My wife allowed me to spend the night on the couch and take a shower. However, I had to leave the next day.

The next morning I was out in the front of my house wondering how I was going to pick up my trailer and make it to camp with the brakes as bad as they were when my next-door neighbor came over to say hi. He and his wife were both Christians and I had done some youth events at the church where he and his whole family attended. He told me he knew I had been gone for a long time because Cheryl had told him. I shared with my neighbor my current dilemma. I had to get to camp because I was doing worship, but my brakes were in bad shape. He told me, "Let's go over to the auto repair store and fix your brakes." He said he would pay for it. I can't tell you how grateful I was for help.

We got the brakes and I went back home to say goodbye to my children before I left again. It just tore me up, but I had no choice but to go. I told my family that I would call them soon. I drove back to Cottonwood, got my trailer and headed for the camp, which was about an hour and a half away in the forest of Northern Arizona. I had just come down this large hill going the speed limit, which was sixty-five miles per hour, and I made the turn to the youth camp which was set back a few miles off the road. It was a public camping area, so I was driving very slowly over the paved street. As I was making the last turn to camp I had to cross a one-way bridge spanning a riverbed. It was only about forty yards long. Just as I was going over the bridge and making my turn to the camp, I heard this loud bang and then the sound of dragging metal. I had only been going five miles per hour over the bridge, but my trailer was finally finished. The frame was cracked and broken and I was only able to drag it about ten yards further down the road before that was it. My thoughts went back to the hill that I had just come down at sixty-five miles per hour. What if the frame had snapped then? It would have been over for my van, my trailer and me. I thanked the Lord for my safety and I dragged the trailer as far over to the side of the road as I could. It was raining and getting dark. I locked everything up and then started to walk the last mile to the camp.

28

IT'S GOING TO EXPLODE

~

Wow! I should have never made it that far. I knew Pastor Greg would be wondering what happened to me. I had done so many camps with him and his family, and he knew I would get there somehow. As I was walking, I was thinking of all the Divine appointments the Lord had set up for me over the past month. The interesting question was: Would they have ever happened if I had just stayed in Phoenix? I think Divine appointments can happen everyday of our lives if we are tuned into what the Lord has for us to do. But we must be willing and obedient to follow God's calling or who knows who and what we might miss.

It was almost totally dark when I arrived at the camp. I had been here many times over the years and it was one of my favorites. I went into the small chapel where Pastor Greg and the young people were gathered and said hello. They were glad to see me and I was more than glad to see them. They said, "Are you going to get set up and do worship?" "Well," I told them, "my van and trailer are down the road." I explained what had happened as I crossed the bridge and how God had brought me through so many challenges over the past few weeks. I was straight up honest with them. That is the way we need to be. The twelve young people, eight of whom were Native American, were all from group homes run by Pastor Greg. This was by far the smallest camp we had ever done together, but that didn't mean it would be any less powerful. And it was great to know I was going to be in one place for a few days.

The next day was Tuesday, August 8th. That morning, a few of us went down to my van and trailer with some tools to see if we could somehow fix the trailer up enough to get it to camp. We took some 2x4 planks of lumber and some rope and made splints around the cracked tubing of the trailer. We got it up about two inches off the ground and slowly drove the van at about three miles per hour back to camp. It took what seemed like all morning but we did it. Then we had morning service and worship. The power of God was so strong that the youth did not want to leave the presence of the Lord, so we stayed in the chapel until lunch was served. The next few days were full of exciting times with the Lord.

On the last day, I felt something different was going to happen. I told Pastor Greg that we were going to have visitors. He told me that we were supposed to be the only ones in the camp until Friday morning when we were to leave. I told him that all I knew was that we were going to have visitors. At lunchtime, I was talking to one of the camp directors and he told me that they had forgotten to tell us that a high school from Phoenix was going to be arriving that day. It wasn't a church group; it was a high school bringing sixty young people as part of a leadership program. They would be arriving in the afternoon but he told me they wouldn't bother us that night because they didn't need the chapel until the next day and we would be leaving in the morning. I thought to myself, "I still think there is more to it than that."

It was our last evening in the chapel on Thursday night and the Lord was moving among the young people in a powerful way. I was up on this small stage area playing worship music and all of the young people we had brought were on their faces in the presence of the Lord. Then I saw seven other young people walk into the chapel. I like to bring my own lighting to set the atmosphere for worship and we had the lamps set down low. As they walked in, they looked over at Pastor Greg and he just nodded his head and smiled at them. All seven of them joined in worship with their hands lifted. There were two boys that stood right in front of the speakers and they started to yell loudly. It was really amazing. They were yelling at the top of their voices into the speakers. Their cries were, "God, save our generation!" "God, set our generation free!" "God, save our friends!" I just turned up the music louder and they yelled louder, falling to their knees and petitioning God to move on their school, their friends, their families, and this country. This continued for over an hour and we had already been worshiping the Lord for more than two hours before they had arrived. When the night had come to an end, the seven new boys came up to me and asked, "Will you be here every night?" I told them that our group had to leave in the morning. They told me they had never experienced anything like that at their church. I gave them my card and said, "I'm sure we will meet again soon."

The next morning we packed everything back into my van and trailer. I told the camp director that I would return for it as soon as I could find someone to weld my trailer back together. Little did I know that would be harder than I thought. But for now, it would be safe at the campground. I drove back to Cottonwood with everyone. Pastor Greg said that I could stay at his house and offered me a comfortable couch to sleep on. The next few days I stayed in Cottonwood and tried to find someone to fix my trailer. With no luck, I drove back to the camp in Payson and called different people there, but no one could help me. It was crazy. Even the camp director said it was strange. Well, maybe it was just supposed to stay there for a while. I told them I would take as much of my gear as I could, so I packed whatever would fit into my already overloaded van and drove back to Cottonwood.

Pastor Greg invited me to go to the church that he and his family were attending in Cottonwood. So, on Sunday morning I went to this church called Emmanuel Fellowship. When I walked in, they had just started worship and the presence of the Lord was heavy in the house. I loved it. There were over three hundred fifty people in the church that morning and as the worship service continued, I told Pastor Greg that I had a word for this pastor. Greg just looked at me like, "Here we go." I told Pastor Greg, "Come with me." He said, "Bobby, they are in the middle of worship." I said, "I know. Come on." The pastor was on the stage worshipping with the worship leader and the choir. I told Pastor Greg again, "Come on." So he reluctantly walked to the aisle with me. As I walked down the aisle, I thought that Pastor Greg was right behind me, but as soon as I got down to the front and turned around, there he was in the back smiling at me. Oh well. I walked over to the stage, took the pastor's hand and said, "I'm Bobby Dendy and that is my friend back there. I have come to your church for the first time, and the Lord told me to tell you that this church is about ready to explode. It could happen in the nursery, the children's department, anywhere, but it is going to explode."

I said a few other things, too, but I can't remember them. Pastor Frank still had my hand and smiled at me. I turned and walked back up the aisle. When I got back to where Pastor Greg was, I jokingly said, "You chicken." He just laughed. We had known each other for sixteen years and he knew that when God sends me, I'm gone. I watched as Pastor Frank continued to worship with the worship leader, the band, and the choir. The worship leader was really powerful and the band and choir were incredible. I was thinking, "For a church this size, the talent and anointing are so strong." After the worship was over and the announcements had been made, the pastor told the congregation that a man who he had never met before had come up to him during worship and prophesied over this house exactly what had been prophesied over this church for the past few years and even more so in the last few months. "He told me, 'This church is about ready to explode. It could happen in the nursery, the children's department, anywhere, but it is going to explode.'" With that announcement, there went up from the congregation a loud roar and praise. I thought, "WOW, this house could go up at any moment." I listened as Pastor Frank preached that morning and a thought came to me, "This man needs to be on TV. He is not a pastor; he is a true shepherd with the gifting of a pastor and more."

After service, I waited around with Pastor Greg. When the church was almost totally empty, Greg asked, "What are you waiting for?" I told him, "You will see." Just then Pastor Frank came up to me smiling and said, "Ok, who are you?" I told him that I was a friend of Pastor Greg's and that he had invited me to the service. Pastor Frank said, "Will you be staying long in Cottonwood?" I told him, "I have been on a journey of brokenness from the Lord and I'm hoping to be restored to my family soon in Phoenix." He told me, "You were right on this morning with that word from the Lord. The same exact word has been spoken over Emmanuel Fellowship for the past few years and as little as a few months ago from a very highly respected prophet to the church." I told him that I would stop by anytime I was in town. I also told him that the worship and sermon that he taught were exactly what I needed to hear. After church, I ate lunch with Pastor Greg and told him that I had to go see my friends, Kim and Jim, on my way to Lake Havasu. I had to tell them some of the journey that I had been on. I wasn't sure why, but I had to go. Greg gave me some money for going to the camp. He said, "I know it's not much." I told him, just as I had told everyone else, "It's enough." It seemed whatever I received was just as much as the Lord wanted me to have.

29

TELL YOUR STORY

~

My friends' RV Park was over an hour away and Lake Havasu was going to be another three hours after that. When I made it to Kim and Jim's, I shared with them a couple of stories. They said, "Somehow, God will use this to help people and to restore your family." They gave me some money for my trip to Havasu, so now I was confident that I would at least make it there. They asked if I wanted to stay overnight but I told them that I had to go. I was really tired but the Lord was pushing me to go right then. They understood. After all that I had been through, we knew that if the Lord said I had to go, it would be okay.

I drove to Lake Havasu and found a place to sleep right next to a truck stop just outside of town. I was thinking, "Lord, what is up with this?" Lake Havasu in August is over 115°F in the day and well over 100°F past midnight. So here I was in my packed van sitting straight up with the window down trying to sleep. Why did I have to stay here? One thing started to become clear as the Lord would wake me at all hours of the day and night. I was being positioned to be at the exact place at the exact time that I needed to meet someone who the Lord wanted me to meet.

I got up early as always. I had hardly gotten any sleep. It was 5:30 A.M. and time to go into the city of Lake Havasu. I went to McDonalds for breakfast and then on to a beautiful park by the waters edge. I had been in this same park a few years earlier. It is called London Bridge Park. A large lake surrounds it and there is a waterway channel that goes under the world's famous London Bridge. I spent a few hours there, walking and praying, and then I left for the radio and TV station that my friends own and run. It is a radio/TV station that was heard in many other cities including Las Vegas, Bullhead City, Kingman, etc. It had been about a year since I'd seen my friends. I knew the Lord was up to something. When I arrived at the station I reunited with my friends and spent the next two hours sharing a few of the journeys I had already been on. After I was done sharing with them, they gave me their corporate gas card and said, "Bobby, go fill up your van and come back. We would like to talk to you some more." When I got back from the gas station, they said, "Bobby, when you get a chance, you need to write down some of these journeys so that we can tell your story on radio and TV." I told them that when the time was right, I would be back. My friends' dedication to the Lord and Christian radio/TV has been an inspiration to me. They don't make a move until they have sought the Lord for direction and wisdom.

30

DO THE NEXT THING

~

I decided that I was going to head back to Phoenix to see my children for a few hours. I could still hear that sound coming from one of my back tires, but I couldn't find anything there when I got back to Phoenix. So, I went to see one of my Christian friends who worked in the automotive repair area at a car dealership. I shared with him a few of the journeys that I had been on and asked if he would also take a look to see if he could see where that metal sound by my wheel was coming from. We both looked under my van but couldn't find anything. He mentioned, "Bobby, your van is almost sitting on the ground." I said, "I know. I have to use my side mirrors to see when I drive because everything is packed to the ceiling." Then he asked me what I planned to do next. I told him that I was still trying to get a hold of the owner of the stone company in Northern Arizona. I also told him that my wife wouldn't let me live at home. She wanted me to get a full-time job, give up this ministry dream, and live away from home for a year while helping to support the family. And then, if I could prove to them that they were first, I could come home. My friend looked at me with concern. He could see that I was exhausted and at the point of breaking down. He said, "Bobby, I will pray for you and your family. I believe God is going to heal you on these journeys." Journeys? *Wait a minute,* I thought. *I'm done with the journey. I want to go home... but what home?* I said goodbye to my friend and went to see my wife and my children. They were all very cold and distant to me, except my youngest, Casidie. Being autistic, it was even harder for her to understand why I was away from home and it was tearing her up just as much as it was my wife and my other two girls. I spent a little time with her and then said goodbye as she cried and pleaded with me not to go. I drove away from my house crying. I felt like a stranger in my own home.

I decided to go back to Cottonwood. I could stay with Pastor Greg for a while as I tried to reach the owner of the stone company. The next few days in Cottonwood brought a little rest to my journey. I had a couch to sleep on and friends around me, but my heart was broken and every minute I was thinking of my family and how to get home.

On Thursday, August 17th, the Lord sent me to talk to Pastor Frank. I had only talked to him one other time and that was in the service the previous Sunday. I went to the church office and asked if I could speak with Pastor Frank. The church secretary replied, "You can see him now." I went into his office and sat down. Pastor Frank looked at me and asked, "How can I help you?" I said, "Pastor Frank, God is not impressed with your preaching." He just looked at me stunned. I said, "He is impressed with your heart." I told him, "You have a heart after God like David and you are a shepherd." I continued, "There are many pastors, but very few true shepherds in the body of Christ." I said, "I watched how you worshipped among the people. God sees your heart." Pastor Frank thanked me for the word and asked me what I was going to do next. I told him about the stone company and how I was still unable to make a connection there. I also mentioned the large Christian DJ music Festival in Traverse City, Michigan that Darryl had told me about. I felt I was supposed to go, but it was over two thousand miles away. I told him, "I have already been on some long journeys, but if God wants me to go, I will." Pastor Frank told me he would pray for my family and me. I told him I would probably see him on Sunday at service and make my decision whether to leave or stay on Monday.

I got on a computer at a friends house in Cottonwood to look up some information about the festival in Traverse City. My friend Darryl was right. It was what I had been waiting for for sixteen years. It was going to be an incredible event, but how was I going to get there? My trailer was broken and still in the youth camp in Payson. I had all of my sound gear, clothes, etc. packed into my van and it was sitting on the ground like a low rider car. I took out my U.S. atlas and plotted a route that would take me to Traverse City. Well, if God did ask me to go, my drive would take me right through Kansas City, Missouri. I had always wanted to go to The International House of Prayer (IHOP) there. People from all over the U.S. and around the world would go there to visit, and they also had a university equipping students as missionaries in whatever area they were called. As I looked at the map of the United States I thought, "Traverse City is a long way from Cottonwood. I would need some serious confirmation from the Lord for me to go."

Sunday service at Emmanuel Fellowship was powerful. I went to all their services that day, two in the morning and one in the evening. Of course, the message was the confirmation I needed to go. Telling my wife was going to kill me. She was expecting me to call any day to tell her that I had a job with this stone company or that I had found a job in Phoenix, not that I was going on another Christian concert vacation. I had called Pastor Dorie and my friend Darryl to let them know that I was going to Traverse City, Michigan, somehow. Darryl said he knew that I was supposed to be there. I told them that if I left the next day, I could get there in time for Friday's opening events, but that I still didn't have much money and wouldn't get far. Pastor Dorie said she would pray and tell her husband, Jeff.

On Monday, I went to a public laundromat to wash my clothes. After I finished my laundry, I got a call from Pastor Jeff. He told me he had talked to his wife the day before and she informed him of my plans to go to Michigan. Pastor Jeff said, "Bobby, I think this is a mistake. How are you going to get across the country?" I didn't tell him that the trailer was broken and sitting in a youth camp in Payson, leaving my van overloaded and making strange sounds. I told him, "I know you don't understand, but someone is waiting for me." He said, "What?" I explained again that there were people waiting for me and that I had to go. He said, "Bobby, I just can't support what you're doing. I can't see how this is bringing healing to your family." I told Pastor Jeff, "My wife wants me to be out of the house for a year with a full-time job and then she will see from there. Now, the owner of the stone company won't be back for a few weeks and all I can tell you is that I have to go, people are waiting for me." Again he said, "I believe you're making a big mistake." I knew that I couldn't explain all that I had been through to Pastor Jeff over the phone and I didn't have the time either. He said, "I will pray for you and your family," and with that he hung up.

I was still sitting in my van at the laundromat with my head on the steering wheel crying out to God, "What do You want me to do?" I respected Pastor Jeff so much and he had done so much to help me and my family and our ministry to reach youth. I felt totally alone. I cried for half an hour and then I remembered something Pastor Jeff had taught me about life when you feel overwhelmed. He had told me, "Don't look at the whole thing that is before you all at once. Just ask God to help you do the next thing. Do that next thing and then after that is done, again, just do the next thing." *Ok Lord, I will do the next thing and go to Traverse City, Michigan.*

I went back to Pastor Greg's house and told everyone goodbye and that I would keep them updated while on my way to Traverse City.

PART II

~

In writing out this journey I've come to the part that I knew wouldn't be easy for me. For over a year, I have had many people ask me to write about these journeys and I've tried to start this book a hundred times but with no success. As I got closer to this point in the story, I wasn't looking forward to reliving it again. But I knew that if it could help at least one person, I had to do it. On my first journey I didn't have a micro-cassette recorder to record some of my thoughts and feelings as they occurred, but for this part of my travels, my friend Darryl gave me his recorder and said, "You might want to record some things as you go." I know full well that I'm writing this story now in God's timing. It's just that listening to and revisiting my thoughts and emotions from the tapes of these journeys has proven to be really hard and emotional for me.

My friend, Les, told me that it was going to be important to capture all that I have been through so that I could write this book. Les and his wife Linda are truly amazing friends. They work for and run a company called Metropolitan Audio and Visual. This is a company that Linda's sister and brother-in-law own. Les and Linda and this company have done more to help me, and my ministry, than you could imagine. They have given me over sixty thousand dollars worth of production equipment over the past four years to help me to reach people with a positive message of Hope and Jesus Christ. They said, "Just keep going, Bobby. One day soon you will have the money to pay us for this equipment." That was four years and many events ago. I could not have done what I have done without their trust and belief in me. This book is in big part due to them pushing me to tell you these stories.

31

I MADE IT

~

It was now Monday, August 21st. I had four days to travel over two thousand miles to Traverse City, Michigan. It was going to be a long travel day for me. I was hoping to make it from Cottonwood, Arizona to Santa Fe, New Mexico that day. It was going to take over twelve hours. I plugged on and made it to just outside of Santa Fe. I slept in the van for about four hours before continuing on my way. The next day, Tuesday, August 22nd, I stopped at a gas station in Colorado Springs and gave one of the ladies working there my card with the poem *Happytown* written on the back. She read it and liked the poem. She said, "This poem is so true." Then she asked, "Where are you going?" I told her, "Traverse City, Michigan." She told me she had been there many times. She said her brother had died unexpectedly two weeks ago and that he had lived in Michigan. I told her that I would pray for her and her family. She said, "Thanks for the card and the poem and have a safe journey." There was that word again, journey.

I had called my sister-in-law Robin to tell her I was going through Denver, Colorado and wanted to see her. She lived just outside of Denver, on my route to Kansas and beyond. When I got to her town, we met at one of the stores. She asked me what I would need for the journey. I told her and we got a tent, sleeping bag, and all kinds of snacks for my trip as well as a full tank of gas. I gave her a hug and then off I went. It was already 5:00 P.M. and I would have to drive through the night to make up some ground. I slept for only a few hours at a rest stop outside of Topeka, Kansas. I can't tell you how many times I almost fell asleep at the wheel. I wanted to stop, but I just couldn't until the Lord let me. I was totally exhausted, but I woke up early again on Wednesday and drove as far as I could go. I had to make it to the International House of Prayer (IHOP) in Kansas City, Missouri. I was on the interstate, forty five miles away, when my low fuel light came on meaning I only had two gallons of fuel in the gas tank and I had been averaging twenty miles a gallon. You do the math. I was praying hard. They were doing some construction on the freeway and there was no shoulder, so if I ran out of gas, I would be holding up traffic on the whole freeway. I kept looking for an exit to get off, that way if I did run out of gas I would be stuck on a side street. I finally came to one and made it off the freeway and parked at a small convenience store. I went to go into the store just as an elderly man was walking out. I asked him if he knew where IHOP was and he answered that is was about thirty-five blocks away. He gave me directions and I thanked him before starting on my way again. As I drove away I realized that I hadn't told him that I was out of gas or asked him for help. I was way past empty on my gas gauge for the van. Oh well.

My mind raced as I thought about what I would see when I finally arrived at IHOP. I had heard so much about this place with 24/7 worship that had been going on for almost seven years. I was certain that it was going to be packed with all these Christians and that I would be able to get more help than I could possibly use. I was also looking forward to some rest and something to eat. I only had a little change left. I had spent almost everything I had on the toll freeways to get here, using the last seven dollars for gas at my last gas stop before IHOP. As I was driving through the residential streets, I started to think, "How in the world did I get here?" It felt like I was in one long dream and at any moment I was going to wake up. As I turned down the last road leading to IHOP, I was praying, "Please let me make it into the parking lot somehow." When I spotted the IHOP sign a few blocks away, I knew that I had made it. I pulled into the parking lot. The buildings before me housed various parts of the IHOP base. There were training rooms, a café, and a bookstore next to the main prayer and worship building. I parked and just sat in my van for a while. It was around 3:00 P.M. and the parking lot was about half full. There was a gas station on the other side of the building and a liquor store about twenty-five yards away. I thought it was interesting that there would be a liquor store so close. It even shared the same entrance as IHOP on one side of the building. I just sat in the van exhausted from the trip and the stress of having no gas in a place that I had never been. I had only a couple of bottles of water and an apple left to eat, but I made it.

32

PLACE OF WORSHIP

~

I went inside the main entrance to the worship chapel. There was a reception area with a receptionist available to answer questions and a guest book for visitors to sign in. I started to walk over to sign in and I heard the Lord tell me not to. Just then one of the side doors to the chapel of worship opened up and two college age students came out. I went inside to find hundreds of chairs set up with a large sound booth area in the middle of the room. I was standing in the back and as I looked up front beyond the sound booth, I could see the stage with the musicians playing and singing. There were rooms behind me and on both sides running half the distance of the main sanctuary. Some of the rooms were titled "Healing Rooms" while others were prophetic teaching and prayer rooms. The main area was less than half full and I noticed that most of the people were on lap top computers. I assumed that since they had a school as part of this ministry, they were doing homework or assignments for class. The singers and musicians did a harp and bowl type of worship and occasionally they would put up the lyrics to the songs. There were TV monitors placed throughout the building. It was also much more comfortable inside compared to the humid conditions outside. I sat in one of the chairs with my bible and listened to the worship music. When the worship team changed they would leave one person playing guitar or keyboard while the next worship team came up to join them. Then the person playing the guitar or keyboard would leave the stage and the remaining worship team would take over for two hours.

As the night went on, I watched the different worship teams and other volunteers come and go. When I got up to find the restroom I came across the schedule for the worship teams posted in the hallway near the front desk area. It listed the leaders of each team along with the musicians and singers and also the names of the prayer volunteers and team leaders. What I didn't understand was that if the presence of the Lord was supposedly so strong, why were all of these people leaving after their two hour set and not staying for the next worship team? I went outside to see where everyone was and many of them were either at the café or they had already gone home.

I went back inside to pray. I noticed that there was never anybody up in the open area in front of the stage. There was a large area for an altar where people could get on their faces or kneel but people just sat in their chairs. Sometimes someone might be standing or lifting their hands, but mostly sitting, many of them on their computers. I understand the revelation you can get while simply sitting in the presence of the Lord, but I had just been expecting the presence of the Lord to be overwhelming and it wasn't. I have been in the presence of the Lord at times when everyone was on their faces and the presence was so strong you could hardly move. It was at these times that healings happened, deliverances happened, along with many other miracles.

I continued to watch through the night as worship teams and prayer teams came and went. People aren't allowed to sleep in the church, as they are open 24/7, so I went outside at 1:00 A.M. to sleep in my van. It was raining and very humid. I think I slept for about an hour then I went back into the church. When I sat down, I noticed a young man sitting three rows in front of me. He had his laptop open and his headphones in, jamming away. I could see from his laptop that he was on some sort of music program. I went over and handed him my business card then went back to sit down. He looked at my card, turned around, smiled and gave me the thumbs up sign. A few minutes later he came over to me and asked if we could talk in the hallway. He said, "No one is allowed to talk in the worship and prayer room." I told him, "I understand." So we went out into the hall. He asked me where I was from. I told him, "Phoenix, Arizona." He asked, "So, you are a DJ?" I answered, "I have been a DJ for over twenty eight years and right now I am on my way to a Christian music festival with DJs from around the world." I told him that the festival was in Traverse City, Michigan and that I had come this far and had not yet been released to go any further by the Lord. I asked him where he was from and he answered that he had come from New Jersey and told me about the many miracles that brought him to Kansas City. I also asked him about the music program he was using on his laptop. He explained to me that the Lord had told him he was going to be used in Hip Hop music. I asked him if he had any training in producing beats and music. He told me that he didn't, that he would just hear the music in his head. The Lord had made a way for him to get the laptop and the music software to produce music. I told him that the program he was using was one of the top programs used in the best recording studios around the world. He told me that he knew that because many of the musicians he had met at IHOP had told him it was the most advanced program that was available. I asked him how long it had taken him to learn the program. He answered that he had prayed and that the Lord then downloaded it to him in five minutes. I said, "Are you serious?" He said, "Yes. You can ask anybody around." He then told me that he had already produced a few songs and was working on a new song right at that time. I told him that I knew people who had been working on that particular program for over a year and still didn't have it down. He went on to tell me that he had been at IHOP for six weeks and it had changed his life. I asked him if in the six weeks that he had been there, had he ever seen anyone at the altar on his or her knees or down on their face? He said no. Most everyone there was a student or a volunteer for the two-hour worship sets. He told me that they would sometimes get guests that had to register at the front desk. We went on to talk about the Lord and music and he asked me how long I would be staying. I told him, "Not long. I have to make it to Michigan by tomorrow." It was now Thursday and the festival opened the next day.

33

YOU CAN'T KILL A DEAD MAN

~

It was now about 4:00 A.M. and I went back into the worship room and sat down to pray. I asked the Lord for some kind of sign to go on. I was beyond tired and the enemy kept telling me, "What are you doing? You are out in the middle of nowhere. You can't talk to anyone or let anyone help you. You have made a big mistake."

I was thinking about my friends, John and Lisa, from Texas. The Lord had used them many times to encourage me and pray for me. Then, around 9:00 A.M., I got a call from John telling me that the Lord had woken Lisa up with a word for me. She got on the phone and told me what the Lord had told her. It was amazing and just what I needed to hear. I thanked the both of them and told them I would talk to them soon. I still wasn't allowed to talk to anyone or ask for help, but I felt the Lord encouraging me.

By the afternoon I hadn't had anything to eat and only water to drink so apparently I was fasting. I was praying and asking God, "What do you want me to do?" I listened and I heard a message about repentance. That we were to turn our hearts toward our children and then our rebellious children would turn their hearts back to their fathers. The Lord told me that we were to sell our stuff. People have so much stuff in storage sheds, garages... you name it! Sell our stuff. And we were to plant all we have into our children. He told me that they are the last ones. And He told me the most important thing we needed to do was to repent. I had been in Kansas for over a day and the worship and love for the Lord that had established this place was amazing. If the young people didn't love the Lord, they wouldn't have come here to be trained. But something was missing. It was repentance. I had heard worship and interceding prayer, but they weren't of repentance for the nation or for this generation. I kept praying, "Lord, who am I supposed to talk to before you let me leave?" Darryl had called me and told me that the festival was looking for a praise and worship DJ to open the festival. I told him, "If I drive through the night and all day tomorrow, I can make it, but the Lord hasn't let me go from here yet." The Lord was keeping me there for a reason.

During one of the afternoon sessions, a gentleman got up and started praying and petitioning God as the musicians were playing. He was petitioning the Lord for revival. He was saying to the Lord, "You promised us seventy thousand souls." It was really powerful. I had heard many people pray during the different sessions but this was different. I was way in the back on my face between the chairs and the Lord said, "Get up and go tell that man you have the answer to his prayer." So I got up and looked to see who was praying and I saw a man in a blue shirt just behind one of the pillars. He continued praying and asking God for revival. The Lord told me again that He had an answer to his prayer. We needed to repent. We needed to be broken before the Lord; then He would send revival.

I waited about fifteen minutes and then I started to walk up front to find the man in the blue shirt that was praying. I had been there for a day and a half and I hadn't registered as a guest, so I wasn't allowed to talk to anyone, and I knew the team leaders and others were wondering who I was as I walked to the front. A couple of the team leaders in the front started to walk toward me as I got closer but they were stopped right at the edge of the aisles and I just walked by. When I got to the front, I saw the man in the blue shirt sitting in a chair with his eyes closed. As I approached, he suddenly fell to his knees and put his face into his bible on the floor. I just stood there waiting for him to get done praying. I looked around and noticed that the team leaders were still standing at the edges of the aisles, frozen. They weren't moving, just staring at me. When the man lifted his head up and sat back in his chair, I introduced myself. I said, "I'm Bobby Dendy from Phoenix, Arizona. I have been here for over a day and the Lord has kept me here and hasn't released me yet. I have a multi-media ministry to teens, pre-teens and college students and I would like to talk to you for a few minutes, if it's okay." He said, "What would you like to talk about?" "Well," I said, "it's kind of an answer to your prayer." So he opened up one of the doors in the front by the stage and said, "Come on in." I went inside and started telling him how awesome I thought this place was. The training was amazing and the young people and the worship teams were phenomenal and the harp and bowl worship was great, but there was just one thing missing. I explained to him that God had been having me bring this message to many different pastors all over the country: It needs to quit being about us and start being about our children. We need to take and pour all our resources into our children. We need to repent. We are a prideful country and we are arrogant. We have not humbled ourselves before the Lord and that's why we don't have revival. We have everything else, but we don't have revival because we are not willing to humble ourselves before God and repent and be broken.

I went on to tell him, "I have really been broken." Then I said to this gentleman, "I'm sorry, I didn't get your name, sir." He said, "My name is Mike Bickle." All of a sudden it hit me; this is the Founder of IHOP. I could tell by the look on his face when he told me his name that he knew I hadn't known who he was because he could see the shocked look on my face. I told him, "I didn't know who you were. I was on my face in the back of the room and the Lord told me that the man who was praying, the man that had a heart after Him, was the man I was to talk to." Mike then told me that this was the only session where he was the leader and after this he had to catch a plane right away because he was responsible for the 'One Thing' conferences all over the country. The one in Atlanta was starting that night and he had to go. He looked at me and said, "Bobby, that was a word from the Lord to me and to this house. Thank you for being obedient." I said goodbye and went back to my seat. The whole time I was walking back down the aisle I was thinking, "Lord, you are so funny. That was a nice move on your part." I kept thinking, *You can't kill a dead man*, and I was surely dead or dying to myself so that the Lord could use me however He wanted to.

I spent the rest of the day in the prayer room. I hadn't eaten anything in a day and a half and I was still not allowed to talk to anyone. I went out to my van around 1:00 A.M. to try and sleep for a couple of hours but again it was raining and really humid, so I went back into the church and laid down to read my bible and fell asleep. I'm sure I had been snoring when one of the volunteers woke me up and said, "I'm sorry, sir, you can't sleep here." So I got up and walked around and tried to wake up. It was now 4:00 A.M. I thought to myself, "I have really only slept about six hours in the past two days, plus all the driving to get to IHOP." It was Friday morning, August 25th, and there was no way I could make it to Michigan by that night. I still didn't have any money, and the Lord hadn't released me yet. I told the Lord, "I would sure like to go today." I didn't have a drop of gas and I had a total of seventy cents left. The Lord still wouldn't let me talk to anyone or ask anyone for help or to borrow money. So, I looked at a map and found the closest major grocery store that would have a Western Union about ten miles away. I decided I was going to get out of there. I would walk to this grocery store and wait there until someone wired me money.

So, I started walking. It was sunny out and extremely humid. I got about two and a half miles and thought, "What in the world am I doing?" So I turned around and walked back. I'm sure I smelled really good by then. I hadn't showered in four days, although I cleaned up in the bathroom the best I could. When I got back to IHOP I was truly spent. I said, "Lord, if You're not going to let me ask anybody for help, what do You want me to do?" The Lord told me to take my seventy cents and go to the gas station that was next door to IHOP. There were two Middle Eastern men who owned and ran the gas station. So I got into the van and prayed I could make it thirty yards away.

I pulled up to pump two and went inside the gas station thinking, "This is crazy!" I told the guy behind the counter, "I know this is going to sound crazy, but I need seventy cents on number two." He said, "Seventy cents?" I said, "Yes, I have to get a place where someone can wire me money to help me." I explained, "I'm on a journey traveling across the country." He asked, "You have no money?" I said, "No, I don't have any money. Just seventy cents." He said, "I'll put five dollars in the tank for you." I told him, "Thank you so much." I was so excited. Now I would have at least enough gas to get to the grocery store that had a Western Union. If something happened and someone called, I could get some help from there. When I got to the store, my friends John and Lisa called to tell me they could wire me some money. It was going to take a few hours because he was at his day job and wouldn't get off work for another few hours. He had fifty dollars he could send. I told the Lord, "I will need at least one hundred and fifty to make it to Michigan." This was the number that was in my head. I drove to the grocery store to wait. It was going to be a few hours but at least I was making progress.

34

PANCAKES & PRAYER

~

I had been at IHOP for two days and the only thing I had eaten was an apple. I was looking forward to finally having a substantial meal. I had been in the parking lot for about half an hour when the Lord had me move the van away from the grocery store and park next to a restaurant. Before I could cut the engine the Lord said, "Not here. Park at the restaurant next to this one." So I backed up and parked behind the other restaurant. I didn't even notice the name of it until I got out of the van. As I looked up I saw the big IHOP sign. The International House of Pancakes one. I thought, "Very funny Lord. You take me from one IHOP to another."

I was moving some things around when I noticed some guy's hand by the back of my van. He was standing behind the van, and I called out, "Hey, how are you doing?" He answered "Good," and continued to stand there looking at the back of the truck, at my license plate and then at the "Not of This World Production" logo on either side of the vehicle. I asked him, "Do you like the van?" He said, "Yes." I told him that I had come from a long way away. "I'm from Phoenix, Arizona." He said, "We came from a long way, too," and just then I noticed his accent. His wife and three sons were walking up to their car which was parked next to mine. I said, "Where are you from?" He said, "Norway." His wife put the boys, who looked to between the ages of three and seven, in the car. He asked me, "So, what do you do?" I told him, "I have a ministry to teens, pre-teens and college students and I am traveling across country on this journey the Lord has put me on." He told me he knew all about journeys. I asked him, "What are you doing here?" He said, "We have been at the International House of Prayer." He explained that they were interning there and would be staying for four months. They had only been there for a week so far. As I started to explain about my journey his wife, who had been standing next to us, was hit by the presence of God. She almost fell over. She held up her arm to show me the goose bumps. The bumps on her arm were as big as BBs. I had never seen goose bumps that big on anybody. I started sharing with her what the Lord had had me doing over the past forty days and shared with them God's word to me that we needed to turn our hearts back to our children and repent. I told them, "I have been at the International House of Prayer for the past few days and the Lord used me to bring a word to Mike Bickle last night." The wife yelled, "Oh!" I looked at her as she held her arms up to show me and then I continued, "It's only going to take one or two people simply lying before the altar because they already have everything else there at IHOP. We have pride and arrogance in our country. We need to be broken before the Lord and then the Lord will send revival. People are crying out for revival, but they are not willing to repent and humble themselves and invest all they have into the children. It is time."

She was standing there listening to me while her husband left and then came back. I hadn't told them anything about my finances or the difficulties I had been facing in that area. The husband said that the Lord had told him to give this to me and then handed me a one hundred dollar bill. I couldn't believe it! With the money from John, there was the one hundred and fifty dollars I had asked the Lord for just hours before. I was so incredibly thankful. I told them, "Let's pray." So I prayed for them and for the direction of the Lord in their lives. They had shared with me the revelation that had brought them here. The wife had gone to a prayer meeting in Norway sponsored by IHOP and the Lord had spoken to her to bring her whole family here. I asked her husband, "How did you know you were supposed to come to IHOP?" He told me, "When she came home from that meeting, she was transformed and I just knew it." They didn't know yet what they were going to do when their internship was over at IHOP. I kept praying for them and the Lord told me He would send revival within a week if people would humble themselves and pray at IHOP. Everyone has their own definition of revival, but I just kept praying for them and their family. When I was done praying, his wife showed me her arms again. I gave them my business card and they told me they would e-mail me. I gave them a hug and then I went back to the grocery store to wait for the money John was sending me. He called back soon after and told me he had gotten off work early and was wiring the money right then. I told him thanks so much. I got the money within half an hour and drove back to the gas station next door to the International House of Prayer. I filled up the gas tank and went inside to talk to the station owner. I thanked him again for the five dollars. I said, "Have you ever been to IHOP before?" He told me that he had gone a few years ago. I told him, "You should go back some time soon." As I was getting ready to leave, he said, "If you ever need help again, let me know. I will help you. I will take care of you." I thought, "That was truly amazing, Lord, to have a gentleman help me like that."

I drove back to the restaurant and enjoyed a wonderful mid-day breakfast. I hadn't eaten in three days, so I had to be careful what I ate. My friend Darryl called me just after I finished and was getting back on the road. Before I had left to go to Michigan, he had given me a CD that he had made me. He had told me to listen to it on my journey. He said, "Bobby, if you listen to some of the top secular music artists, you can hear in their music that they are searching for something to satisfy their soul." He said, "Listen to these different artists on your journey." I had played the CD many times on the way to IHOP and there was one song I just played over and over. The song was 'Give Me a Sign' by a secular rap artist called DMX. Darryl then told me that on Thursday the Lord had had his CD player stuck on that song and he had played it nearly forty five times back-to-back. Darryl said that it was a theme song for what I was going through right then. He said, "You need to play it forty-five times." I told him I would.

35

UNGRATEFUL DUDE

~

Rejuvenated, I drove through the night, sleeping for a couple hours at a rest stop. It was now Saturday morning and I was still on the road. I passed through Indianapolis and continued on my way to Michigan. I drove for hours through the rain. I went through a small town about an hour away from Traverse City and passed a little church with a marquee that read, "A man who can kneel before God can stand up to anything." I turned around and used my cell phone to take a picture of it.

I finally arrived in Traverse City but I couldn't find the music festival. I stopped and asked at a gas station if they could direct me to the music festival. They gave me directions and told me it was just across the bay with the big tents. I thought, *"Big* tents?" I was expecting a couple little tents in a park, nothing really big because, for the most part, the Christian scene doesn't have much on a large scale. However, as I drove around the bay I saw the large tents come into view. I said to myself, "That can't be it." As I got closer to it, I was blown away. It was done so professionally, like a major festival with three stages, large festival banners along the street, corporate sponsors, programs, line-ups, and food and clothing vendors. It was really well done. As I parked my van, I saw a guy walking across the street wearing a festival t-shirt and a VIP pass around his neck. I said, "Hey, are you part of this festival?" He said, "Yes I am." I was so excited. I said to him, "Who is the visionary that has been able to get this done?" He said, "It's my mom." I said, "You're kidding me. Can I meet your mom?" He said, "Yes." So I followed him into the festival. It was free to the public. He introduced me to his mom. She was sitting on a golf cart with one of the security guards. As we walked towards her, I looked around at the festival grounds and noticed they were totally empty. I could see that everything was still quite wet, but now the sun was out and the wind was blowing and that would help to dry things out in a hurry.

I asked his mom what had given her the inspiration to do something like this. She told me that it had been the dream of a high school girl in the area who had passed away. Her father and some other businessmen had come together to put this on. She had read the girl's story and was interested in helping to make it happen. She had done electronic music festivals in the past and actually was very well known for producing one of the largest electronic festivals in the world. As she was sharing all this with me, I began to understand why this was done in such excellence. She then told me that it had rained for three straight days without letting up. She said, "Those who live here say they have never seen anything like the amount of rain that came down the past three day. Today will be the first time any of the artists can actually play." I told her, "God sent me over two thousand miles to be here and what I'm seeing is a dream that I have had for sixteen years come true. Even if there is no one else here, this was definitely for me." She just sat on the golf cart and began to cry. I told her how excited I was to see this done on this level and the need for Christian artists who had come from the secular side to see this type of event take place. I said, "I thank you for stepping out and doing this. I know you didn't get a good turnout because of the rain, but this is a seed this year. Even if it is just for the one, that is what it is all about. If you just encouraged one person or just one that was lost comes to the light and finds Jesus, it's worth it." She nodded and explained, "They wouldn't allow us to have the permit for this event until four weeks ago." She said that it really wasn't enough time, but she had felt it was important.

She went on to tell me how much pressure she was under, with the rain and lack of attendance, and because of the large amount of money that the twelve businessmen had put out to do this. She needed something today and I was that something. I told her I would be praying for her and that things were going to work out fine. Some of the artists were finally going to be able to play that afternoon. Many of the artists who got rained out on Friday were already gone, but they tried to fit a few of Friday's artists in on Saturday. I was able to watch and listen to a few DJs that afternoon and it was great for me, but there weren't many people around, maybe a few hundred, and this festival could easily hold thirty thousand.

Late that afternoon I ran into a DJ that I had met a few years ago. He was excited to see me. He had heard from a DJ friend of ours that I was making my way from Phoenix to Michigan for this festival. I shared with him my journey and the challenges I had faced along the way to get to this festival. I thought, "This is the break I need. I have been on the road for six days without a shower and a bed to sleep in. I'm sure he will offer to let me come to his hotel room and take a shower and get some rest." However, after I shared with him about my financial situation, lack of sleep and desperate need for a shower, he didn't say anything. He told me how this festival could have been run better, how he didn't like the time slot he had or the stage he had just played on, etc. I thought, "Lord, can I just slap this ungrateful dude? Just once?" Darryl and I had had this discussion more than once about the arrogance and pride of Christian DJs and why God had not moved on this genre of music yet and here was a perfect example. I told him the same message the Lord had given me to share with Mike Bickle and other pastors and people around the country. He was so full of himself that he didn't hear a thing. I just walked away from him totally disgusted and grieved. After the last artist played that night, I would be sleeping in my van again. Oh well, I had made it. I would just wait and see what tomorrow would hold.

36

MAYBE FOR THIS ONE

~

I only slept for a few hours in my van and was awake at 4:30 A.M. It was Sunday, August 27th. I drove to a small park that overlooked the bay. It was beautiful. I just prayed for my family and for the direction of this festival. The lady who organized it was really taking a beating over the lack of people and I knew it. The Lord told me to give her one of the crosses I had bought in a Colorado Springs truck stop. It was a little stone cross that had only cost me four dollars. I said, "Lord, this is not a very expensive cross and she dresses really nicely." He said, "Give her the cross and let her know you have been praying for her." I knew, all too well, the warfare that comes with trying to do positive things, trying to open peoples' eyes to the idea that God can use something different to reach the youth, something that the church is not used to, but is relevant to where the youth are at today. She had shared with me yesterday all about the critics in the churches that were coming against her for doing this type of event. I had told her to ask all these critics, if what you are doing is so successful, where are all the youth? They are most certainly not in the church. When I had told her that yesterday, she had smiled at me and said, "Bobby, a news crew was here a few hours ago. I wish we could have put you on TV." Then she had asked me if I wouldn't mind talking to the gentleman whose daughter had passed away and who was the backing foundation that had hired her for this event. She said, "He has been taking so much heat from others because of the cost of this event and because no one is here." I told her that I would be happy to and to introduce me when she got the chance.

A little later that morning I went to take some pictures of the festival and the bay. Boats were already out and it was quite beautiful. The first group, which was a hip hop group, wasn't going on stage until 10:00 A.M., so I walked around for a couple of hours until then. I was standing in front of the main stage; it was just me and another husband-and-wife couple. The hip-hop group went on stage to perform. I stood there and watched them. They were really good. They performed and ministered like there were ten thousand people in front of them. As I stood there, a young woman in her late twenties came up and started talking to me. She told me these were her friends from Detroit. I asked her, "Are you from Detroit?" She answered, no, that she was from New York and was staying with them for a while. She asked me where I was from. When I told her Phoenix, Arizona, she said, "You are a long way from home." I said, "Yes, I am. God brought me here to see this and meet some people. I really am enjoying your friends." She said, "They truly are people who love God and are trying to reach out to a generation that is killing itself." We continued to watch them and when they finished their song they said they would like to call up their friend and sister in the Lord from New York. The lady with me said, "I'll be back in a few minutes," and walked up the stairs to the main stage and joined in on a song with them. I thought, "Wow, this woman is good." God started showing me some things about her while she was up there singing and rapping. When she came down later, she introduced me to one of her friends from the group. I told him that he and his wife, also a member of the band, were awesome. He said that his wife had to go use the phone but would come over in a few minutes. I started to share with them what God had put on my heart for this generation and I could feel the strong presence of the Lord. Then I turned to the young lady from New York and started to tell her what the Lord had showed me about her. I told her that God had a husband waiting for her, that God had set aside a husband for her and that she wasn't to compromise. All of a sudden she fell to her knees and started crying while her friend started laughing. I knelt next to her and said, "The Lord says to wait and put yourself aside because your husband is really, really close." She started crying again and said, "I know you are a prophet from God. I know He has sent you here to talk to me." She kept crying. I'm sure the scene was quite interesting; three people in front of this huge stage, one on the ground crying, me on the ground next to her and her friend standing next to us laughing. We helped the girl to stand up and she told me that she had been in a relationship that she knew God did not want her in. She had been trying to break it off, but she was having such a hard time doing so. She wanted to give the ring back and she knew it was the wrong relationship but she had been fighting with God about it because she was lonely and didn't want to be. So everything I was saying was confirmation. I then talked to her friend and he said, "Everything you said was confirmation," and that was why he had been laughing at her. He explained, "We actually had her move from New York to Detroit to stay with us and get away from this relationship that wasn't right for her." The Lord had me share a few more things and then we started praying together. After a few minutes, she turned to me and said, "Have you eaten yet?" I said, "No, actually I haven't eaten in two days." She said, "Follow me" and we went over to the VIP lunch area. She told the security guard, "This is DJ Bobby D. He doesn't have his pass on him, but he is with me," and the guard said, "Go ahead." They had a buffet set up and the food was great. She said, "Bobby, eat all you want." Believe me, I did.

We talked for another hour and she said, "Bobby, do you think the Lord sent you all the way from Phoenix to talk to me?" I looked at her and said, "Apparently." We both laughed. Then she gave me a hug and said, "We have to go, it's a three-hour drive home." I was thinking, "I wish I only had a three hour drive home." I said goodbye to them and had started walking toward one of the stages when I met the director of the festival again. She was on a golf cart by herself and stopped to say hi. I told her that I had gotten up very early in the morning and had been praying for her and that everything was going to be okay. I told her, "I know it's not much, but I have this little cross that I bought in a truck stop in Colorado Springs and this morning the Lord told me to give it to you." She started to cry. It was just a little black cross made out of stone with a small black string for the necklace. I showed it to her and she said, "Bobby, would you put it on me?" I said, "Sure." She was dressed very nicely with expensive jewelry and here I was giving her a four-dollar stone cross and rope necklace. I reminded her that it is all about the one we reach in life, and if we reach just one, it's worth it. All of what she had done this weekend could be just for one person. She told me, "You can't believe how you have ministered to me this morning and what an encouragement you have been to me. I really needed to hear what you had to say today." Then she looked at me and said that God was going to give me the desires of my heart and it was going to be beyond anything I could possibly imagine. I just smiled at her and she said, "I have some people I would like you to talk to today." I told her to just let me know. She took off on the golf cart and I went back to listening to the different DJs.

I watched as families started to come to the festival, some from church and some from the boardwalk. It was fun to watch them dancing around in front of the stage. They weren't coming by hundreds, but by ones, twos, etc. "You know," I thought, "how interesting it is to watch these people enjoy themselves. If there were thirty or forty thousand people, you wouldn't be able to see each individual person. They would be lost in the crowd." I watched as an eighty-five year old man danced with a teenage girl in front of one of the stages. I talked to quite a few people from the community who told me they thought this was awesome and were thrilled that something positive was happening in their city. They weren't Christians, but they thought it was great that something was available to kids and the family and that it was free. Later in the afternoon, I was visiting with a man who had brought his quadriplegic son to listen to the music. I was talking to his son, Mike. Mike couldn't speak very well, so his father interpreted for me what Mike was saying. I watched as his father danced around his wheelchair and moved Mike's arms for him. I asked his father, "How old is Mike?" He told me, "He is thirty-one years old." I thought back to a friend of mine who had asked me to do some ministry for a group people who were mentally and physically challenged and there were many people there who were paraplegic and quadriplegic. I remember one young man coming up to me and telling me through slurred speech, "Bobby, we can't dance on the outside, but we can dance on the inside!" Watching Mike with his father that afternoon with the sun out and the music playing, I thought, "Maybe this is what it is all about. Maybe this whole event was arranged for Mike and his father, so Mike could have an afternoon of dancing. We don't see it, Lord, but You see it. There are so many things that we don't see because we don't take the time to look or ask." I asked Mike's father if I could pray for Mike and he said sure. I put my hand on Mike's hand and I prayed in Jesus' name that God would touch him and heal him and set him free, however He chose to do that. It was incredible to be able to pray for Mike. Another moment that I got to witness and that was funny to me, and interesting to watch, occurred later that afternoon. One of the DJs was playing at the main stage and there was no one around except for this mom with her little children. Her two and a half year old kept running up to the stage and staring at the DJ. It was funny to see this little boy just staring so intently and then he started to dance. His mom ran up and grabbed him and brought him back, but as soon as she turned to take care of one of the other kids, he was off again running to the stage. Finally she gave up and let him go and he was walking around and dancing. It was so cool to see the freedom he had dancing to the beats with the DJ looking down at him. It was just him and the DJ. I thought to myself, "Was this event just for this little boy?" Maybe. You never know.

37

I KNOW WHAT IT'S LIKE

~

When the festival ended that night, I couldn't find the director. She had my card and I had hers, so I knew I would talk to her someday. Now, how was I going to get back home? I was two thousand miles from home and I had no money, no food, no gas and no one had offered or even asked if they could help me. I decided to drive back into town a little ways and park at the grocery store for the night. There was a gas station right next to the grocery store so I wouldn't have to go far. I had talked to my wife a few days before and, in her eyes, I had definitely gone off the deep end. My wife had already told me that she was thinking of filing for divorce.

The next day I was still in the grocery store parking lot with no food and only a little water. I had been praying and listening to my worship music all day. At about 5:00 P.M. I decided to move the van and found out my battery was dead. Perfect! I pulled out my jumper cables and lifted the hood up on the van. I was thinking, "This won't take long. I'm in a grocery store parking lot and there are people everywhere that can see me with the hood up and cables in hand." No one came over to help. Finally I thought, "I'll just walk up to someone and ask for help." But the Lord wouldn't let me. Oh well. I had been waiting for about half an hour when all of a sudden I saw this older looking white Nissan cutting across the parking lot, driving straight at me. Out jumps this guy about nineteen years old and he asks, "Do you need some help?" I said, "Man, I could use some help." I looked at him and said, "I bet you have been here before, haven't you?" He answered, "I have been stranded on the side of the road a number of times and no one stopped, no one helped me. I know what it is like." I told him, "I really appreciate it." He said, "It's not a problem."

He had seen me from across the parking lot and knew I needed help. He said, "A thought came into my head and told me I needed to help you." He told me his name and I asked him if he lived here. He said no, that he lived in a town about fifty miles away but worked in landscaping. He would drive into town everyday and then drive home. We talked some more and then jumped the van. He asked me what I was doing in Traverse City. I told him that God had sent me across the country for the music festival. Now I needed to get to the next festival and then I still had a few weeks to go before I got back to Phoenix. I told him that I had been praying and asking God for help or to send someone who could help me, but I didn't know how God was going to do it. He said, "How much do you need?" I told him that for the next part of the journey I would need $100. That was all I knew because that was all God had told me at that point. He said, "I have a hundred dollars to give to you." I said, "What?" He said, "Yes." That was what he was doing at the grocery store. He was cashing his check. He said, "Bobby, I'm a Christian man." I said, "I kind of figured something like that." We talked a little longer and then he gave me the money. We went over to the gas station and I filled up the van. I got his phone number and address and told him I would send him the money. He said, "Bobby, you don't need to." I told him thanks again and I drove down the road to a taco place to get some food and then I was off once again. I hadn't eaten in two days and it was good to have food in my stomach. I drove for four hours and then stopped to sleep in the van.

38

SOMEONE IS WAITING FOR YOU

~

I got up early Tuesday morning, went to the neighborhood laundromat, washed my clothes and got back on the road. I was heading through Chicago to Wisconsin and made it all the way to a place called Wisconsin Dells. It was a small town but a huge water park attraction community. I had never seen anything like it. I had been driving all day and arrived there in the afternoon. That evening my wife called. She was so discouraged with me. She told me she was going to file for divorce and then she hung up the phone. I spent a good hour crying. I was sitting on a bench on one of the streets and there were families on vacation walking by me, laughing and talking about the fun they were having. I had my hat on with my head down so no one could see my tears as they walked by. I was on assignment from the Lord; I had to finish no matter what. The Lord had told me to go to a festival in Sioux Falls, South Dakota and I had three days to get there. I went back to my van, in tears, and tried to get some sleep. It was next to impossible. I kept waking up every half-hour.

It was still early when I finally got up and I decided to go downtown to the riverside park area. I found a bench and sat down to pray for a couple of hours. I said, "Lord, I need to get out of here and move on in Your time and Your way." Soon after my phone rang. It was my friend Kim from the rock company. She said she had found a guy who was going to buy a car she had for sale and that she felt the Lord telling her to take ten percent of the sale of the car and give it to me. She said, "I haven't sold it yet, but by faith I'm going to send you $400."

It was just ten minutes earlier that I told the Lord that I would need at least $300 to $400. I was going to need over $100 to get into the festival, $100 for gas, $100 for food for the five-day festival, plus a few miscellaneous items. So, for Kim to call and say that the Lord had told her to send $400 was amazing. Kim said she would wire me the money right away and told me to find a Western Union in the town then call her back. I found one at a small grocery store and gave her a call. She said she would call me when she had sent it.

I had been waiting for almost two hours when I got the call from Kim. She said, "You are not going to believe this." "What?" I asked. She continued on, "Western Union is down in Phoenix and all of Arizona." She had gone to a few places with no luck and when she asked the guy at Western Union, "Are they down in any other states?" he had replied, "No, just Arizona." Kim spent the whole day trying to get the money to me and we finally met with success. By 5:30 P.M. I was able to receive the money and I put gas in the van, got some food, and called Kim to thank her so much for her help. It was Wednesday, August 30th and I was about five hours away from Sioux Falls, South Dakota. The next day they were letting the campers into the festival and then the actual event would start on Friday. I had driven thousands of miles with the same noise coming from my back tire, but now it was even louder. "Oh well," I thought. "I have to make it to the festival." On Tuesday I had been talking to Pastor Dorie from Phoenix. Pastor Dorie had said that when she was praying for me, she felt like the Lord was telling her that I was like Abraham, that I had put my sacrifice on the altar. I had been thinking the night before that I had put my family and my will on the altar. I had promises from the Lord about my wife, Cheryl, and my daughters, Krystyn, Keeley, and Casidie and the rest of my family. I knew it looked crazy to everyone but I couldn't stop now. I had to finish my assignment.

I made it to Sioux Falls early Thursday morning and arrived at the festival around 9:00 A.M. There was no one there yet, so I decided to explore the festival grounds. I went down one of the roads that read "festival camping." It was a tractor-made road that cut right through a cornfield. The whole surrounding area of the festival was farmland. I drove down the road and came to an open area. Since there were no cars or trucks around, I turned around and drove back to the entrance of the festival. I was thinking, "Lord, what do You have in store for me here?"

Earlier that morning I had been at Walmart picking up food and other camping supplies for the festival. I was in the camping section when I got this overwhelming feeling of loneliness and hopelessness. I could hear this voice saying, "What are you doing? You are out in the middle of the country. Nobody is allowed to help you. Your own family doesn't want you to come back home. No one cares, no one understands. You need to leave right now!" I was standing in front of these camping lanterns just looking at them and crying. A man came around the corner to look at the gear and there I was crying. Later I thought, "That guy must have thought 'Wow, this guy sure is emotional about camping gear.'" The man picked up something off one of the shelves and I just stood there continuing to cry. I heard the Lord say, "Someone is waiting for you. You have to go." I said, "Lord, I'm tired and I'm so far from home" and then it hit me again "You don't have a home to go back to." Just then my phone rang and it was Darryl. He asked, "Are you alright?" I answered, "I don't think so. I want to go home, but I can't. Even if I could make it, I don't have a home to return to and I still have one more camp in Window Rock, Arizona. On top of that, the Lord wants me to go to a festival in Sioux Falls, South Dakota. I just can't take it anymore. I'm standing in the camping section of Walmart crying like a baby and I think I just scared one of the customers with my emotional outbreak over lanterns." Darryl asked me, "What is the Lord asking you to do?" I told him, "The Lord says that there are people waiting for me at the festival and I have to go." Darryl said, "So what are you going to do?" I replied, "I don't have a choice."

39

MAYBE IT IS US

~

Later, as I sat out in front of the festival, I thought, "Here I am Lord, please lead me to the people I need to meet." I got out of my van and met a man who was looking for the area where the volunteers were supposed to sign in. I helped him look and we saw a sign on an office door that said Life Light Festival. We went inside and they directed the man to where he needed to go and sign in. They told me that camping check-in started at noon and the volunteers would be arriving by 11:30 A.M. They also mentioned that it was supposed to rain for the next few days so I thanked them and decided I should find a hardware store close by. There was one just down the road and I bought a tarp, a rain poncho, and a small camping table and I had enough money left over for the camping area fee. The festival itself was free.

As I walked out of the store, I was looking at the back of my van and I noticed something sticking out from underneath. I bent down to see what it could be and realized it was a corn husk that must have been sticking up when I drove down the road at the festival. I pulled a few stalks out from under the van and checked for anything else that might be there. As I was looking by the passenger side rear wheel, I couldn't believe what I found. I had been hearing this metal flapping noise for thousands of miles and now I finally knew why. The steel belt in the tire was completely sticking out on the very inside of the tire's tread. It looked like a metal porcupine sticking out of the tire all the way around, with large flaps of tire just hanging there. My heart just sank as I thought about how I had been driving like that for over 4,000 miles. The tire could have unraveled at any moment and I would have been down on the rim. I knew I didn't have enough money for both a new tire and the camping fee, so I decided I would worry about the tire later and prayed all the way back to the festival. When I got back, I found the road that would lead me to the camping area. I pulled behind these two large trucks and got out of my van to talk to them. I told them about my problem and they came over to my van and took a look at the tire. They said that the tire could have come off at any moment while I had been driving, and, at 75 mph, it would have sent my van off the road, out of control. While we were talking, a man driving a jeep pulled up behind us and asked where the RV parking was and whether or not there was any RV parking left. He told me his name and I shared with him my situation. I told him, "If you want, I'll take you to the office and see if we can get you the information you are looking for, but I will have to ride with you." So he said, "Ok."

I got into his jeep and he asked where I was from. I told him a little bit about the journey that I was on and how I had gotten to the festival. We arrived at the office and they told us that the RV parking was full, but that we could still get a site in the tent camping area. As we were driving back to where my van was, he looked over at me and asked, "Bobby, are you born again?" I said, "Yes." He asked me very seriously, "What does it feel like?" He told me he had been raised Catholic along with his wife and his kids. He went on to tell me that recently he had been attending his brother's Christian church. He said that their people clapped and sang and he was really drawn to the joy he saw there. He continued to share that his brother was going to be at this festival and that as he was driving by he had felt really strongly that he wanted to come. He had an RV and he was going to see if he could talk his wife and kids into coming, too. I was thinking, "Lord, this is amazing that You would draw this man here at this time so we could have this conversation between the two of us." As we were talking, people started to arrive for the festival. There were only about ten campers by that time. I told him more about accepting Christ and what it meant to be born again. He gave me his business card and asked me to call him later. I told him I would.

I got into my van, pulled up to the entrance of the camping area and paid for my camping permit. There were only a handful of people there, but I knew it wouldn't be long before it started to fill up. I could already see a long line of cars and campers queued up down the dirt road that led to the camping area. The clouds were getting dark and people were saying it saw supposed to start raining very soon. I quickly set up my tent and just as I had finished, it started to rain. It rained that whole afternoon and into the evening as people arrived and set up their camps. It was still raining when I woke up early the next day. It was getting really muddy. I talked to some of the camping directors and they said that a lot of people hadn't checked into their campsites and that others couldn't get in because of the muddy roads. There wasn't anything open yet at the festival and the nearest store was about a mile and a half away. So I walked through the rain and the mud to the store. When I got to there, I met three farmers sitting inside. They were talking about how much they needed the rain. There had been a terrible draught for months and this rain was an answer to their prayers. They asked me where I had come from and I told them. I told them that I had to have my coffee in the morning, rain or shine, and they laughed and said, "We know." It rained all day Friday and continued into the night. I woke up early again on Saturday to find the rain had finally stopped. Again, I walked down to the store; the muddy conditions were ten times worse than the day before. I met one of the volunteers at the road that led to the festival. He told me that the Executive Board for the festival was having a meeting to discuss canceling the event because people were slipping and falling and the roads were so bad that some couldn't even get in. Thankfully, the rain stayed away and the winds picked up, so they put out a call to the farmers in the area and within an hour there were tractors, back loaders, bobcats, and large construction equipment clearing mud away and moving sawdust and woodchips onto the waterlogged roads. The farmers worked all morning and they were able to open the festival at 2:00 P.M. It had been sunny and windy all day and people started coming by the thousands. It was truly incredible to see all these people arriving for the day's concerts. Maybe the Lord had used the weather to unite everyone to pray in one accord for the rain to stop and the sun to shine.

One of the speaker workshops I wanted to check out was still on when they started to let people in, so I decided to head over. As I was walking through the sawdust, woodchips and soggy ground toward the meeting tent, all of a sudden I saw Ron Luce walking out. I said, "Hey, you look like Ron Luce." He replied, "I am." I said, "I know" and I introduced myself. I told him that I had come to hear him speak and that I was from Phoenix, Arizona. He said, "You came a long way to this festival." I responded, "Yes, it has been quite a journey." I stayed and listened to his seminar on the youth of today. The call on his life to reach young people was so obvious, but the fire and zeal that he had that day seemed stronger than ever. It really was the encouragement I needed. Afterwards he told me that he was going to be on the main stage that night to speak. I had talked to my middle daughter the day before and I really needed something to pick me up. She had called me and told me how disappointed she was with me for not coming home and being a "good dad." All that afternoon, after her phone call, I had felt like I had been stabbed in the heart and the wound seemed to only get worse as the day went on. It was later that afternoon that the Lord led me to a family just a few tents from mine. They asked me about the ministry of Not of This World Productions, after seeing the banner I had put on my tent with my logo on it. I went over to talk with them and they invited me to stay and eat. I shared with them about how the Lord had led me to this festival and told them some of the stories of the past few months. The wife started to cry when I told her about my breakdown in Walmart before I had arrived here and how the Lord had told me there was someone waiting for me. She looked at me and said, "Maybe it is us." She went on to tell me how dissatisfied they were with their church and the leaders there. They were hungry for God and wanted more, but weren't sure exactly what it was that they were after. The family had never been to this festival before and had come from their farming community in Minnesota praying they would find what they were looking for here. I looked at the husband and wife and their two teenage children. They had a daughter and a son and both of them, I could see, really loved their parents. They told me that they were home schooled and really liked it. As I sat there, the Lord started to have me share with them about their lives, what was in their hearts, and the great plans the Lord had for them in the future. I have always loved when the Lord uses me this way. I asked them, as they were crying, if what I was saying was confirmation in their hearts. They said yes. I told them that the Lord was going to use their family to help other families and that they were going to have a powerful ministry to youth. They were both crying as they asked me how I knew all this about them and their family. I told them that the Lord had told me.

We continued talking and the wife told me that the Lord was going to heal my marriage and my family. She told me that they would be praying for us. I told them I would see them later at one of the concerts and then headed back to my tent. I can't even begin to tell you how hard it was to be around all these families and not have my wife and children with me, but I had to go on until the end of my assignment. I was certain that the Lord would put all of this together and it would make sense to me somewhere down the road.

40

FRIENDS FOREVER

~

It was now Sunday, September 3rd and the last day of the festival. I was looking for someone I could borrow a generator from. I wanted to make copies of some of the worship CDs I had produced for the people I had met here at the festival but I needed power to use my CD burner. I ran into the couple that was responsible for the campground I was staying at and I asked them if they had a generator I could borrow. They told me that theirs had gone out the night before and the wife explained that her father-in-law had come by with a brand new Honda generator. It had not been used yet and they offered to let me use it as long as I liked. I thanked them and went back to my tent with the new generator. I hooked up the CD burner and made CDs all day. I missed a lot of concerts, but I wanted to bless some of my new friends with music. It was a lot of fun to deliver the CDs to them that afternoon. I didn't know when I would ever see them again.

I was looking forward to the last concert of the festival. It was going to be The Newsboys. I had seen them live three times and they were always so good. It was going to be a great way to close out the festival with the biggest group and largest crowd. I went a couple of hours before the Newsboys came on. There were a couple other Christian artists that I wanted to see that were performing before them. The crowd was getting bigger by the minute. The largest concert area alone could hold over one hundred thousand people and it was almost full. I was sitting way back up from the stage on this hill and I put my chair down to claim my spot before there wasn't one. As I sat there, a guy came up to greet me and introduced himself. He told me his name was Carl. He said that he was from South Dakota and had been raised on a farm in a small town about an hour from where we were in Sioux Falls. He had a bright yellow hat on that said, "Just a good ole Boy." It was torn up and he had a beard and a mustache and was very thin. Everyone around us was looking at him. He looked like he just stepped out of a movie or old TV show. He wasn't dressed like everyone else and as he talked to me, I could see the light of Jesus in his eyes. He told me none of his friends could make it so he was by himself. We ended up talking for almost an hour. He told me how excited he was to see this many people who love Jesus in one place. He explained that he had been coming to this festival for the past five years and he was amazed to see it growing every year. He talked about how he was only one person, but here he was a part of this gathering of God's people. As I talked to Carl, I could sense that the Lord was doing something. We continued to talk and I told Carl just briefly about what I did and how I had been on the road for a while and heard about this festival. I told him how excited I was to be there. He looked at me and asked, "Bobby, can you believe God would put this here in South Dakota?" During our conversation I noticed a lot of people looking at us. I thought maybe it was the glow of the Love of Christ that was emanating from Carl and me. I wasn't sure but I didn't care. Carl went on to tell me about different farm events he would go to throughout the year that related to farming and livestock and how, although there were a lot of people at these events, it was nothing like this where people gathered for one purpose. I looked at Carl and said, "Imagine what heaven must be like, with millions and millions of people worshiping the Lord." It was so refreshing to talk to Carl and see his childlike love and excitement to be among so many others that loved the Lord.

I watched most of the Newsboys' concert and then decided to go back to my tent early before the rush of people started to exit the festival. While I was at the concert, the Lord had given me some really inspired ideas on lighting for such a large event and some creative designs for staging and multimedia. It was a great experience to be among ninety-five thousand plus people all singing and worshipping with the Newsboys. I was emotionally exhausted. The next day would be Monday and everyone who wasn't pulling out of camp tonight would leave sometime tomorrow. I wasn't sure how I was getting out of Sioux Falls, but I knew God would make a way. He had always been so faithful to help me and I loved the Lord so much. I prayed for my wife and children and tried to rest before the army of Christians leaving the festival started walking by my tent. As thousands left that night, passing by my tent and other tents to get to their cars parked somewhere beyond the campgrounds, I enjoyed listening to their excited voices as they talked of the day's events and the different stages they had attended that day. After a few hours, things quieted down enough for me to catch a couple hours of sleep.

I got up early the next morning and walked to the gas station that was about a mile away for my daily coffee. I ran into one of the farmers that I had met a few days earlier. We talked for a minute and he asked me how the festival had gone and I told him it had been great. When I got back to the festival campground everyone was getting up and packing their vehicles for their rides back home. I stopped by to say hello to Jim, Brenda and their son, Joe. They were in charge of the campgrounds at the festival. They had been true examples of servants of the Lord. I brought them some candy just as I had been doing every morning of the festival. Before the festival began, when I was at Walmart buying supplies, the Lord had had me buy some bags of candy. I didn't understand why at the time, it wasn't the kind of candy I liked, but when I arrived at the festival and had signed in and paid my camping fee I met Jim and Brenda and their son, Joe. Later that first morning, the Lord had told me to bring a bag of candy to Brenda and thank her and her family for their hard work as volunteers for the festival. When I gave the candy to Brenda she got all excited and said, "How did you know this was my favorite candy?" I said, "I didn't know, the Lord told me to buy it. It's not my favorite candy but He told me I was to give it to you." So now it was the last day and I was bringing the last bag of candy to Brenda and saying my goodbyes. They thanked me for the candy and the CDs I had made them and asked me to have a cup of coffee with them and talk for a while.

They shared some of their stories of the festival and the impact it had on their lives every year. They also told me a few stories of their mission trips with the founders of Life Light Festival and how they had gotten involved with the festival. They went on to share how dissatisfied they were with their church. They were so hungry for God and didn't know what to do about it. It was amazing; I had heard the same story all over the country. I asked them if we could pray. I prayed for their family and thanked them for their servant-like hearts and attitudes. Then Jim prayed for me and asked the Lord to bring my family and me back to the festival together one day. It was a sad moment for me to once again make friends and then to leave with so many questions still unanswered as to when or if I would ever see them again. I bid them farewell and then went to say goodbye to the other people I had camped and made friends with. Randy and his wife came by before leaving and said, "I know it's not much but it's all the cash we have on us, so here is sixty dollars to help you get a tire." I told them, "Thank you so much and God bless you." With the sixty dollars Randy had given me plus the fifteen I had, I now had seventy-five dollars for a tire. I waited until all the cars were gone from the campground, finished loading my van and drove up the road. At the top of the road I got out of my van to take a picture. It was hard to leave. I had watched as family after family loaded up to leave and now it was my turn. They were heading home and I was going to look for a tire, unsure of where I would go after that.

41

TIME IS SHORT

~

I drove into town. It was Labor Day and not many stores were open, but I finally came across a tire shop and drove in. The manager came out to look at my tire and was amazed that it hadn't exploded before then. He told me it would be a few hours before they could get to it. I asked him how much a tire would cost. He said the lowest price he could give me with balancing and tax would be seventy-four dollars and ninety-five cents. I told him I only had seventy-five dollars. He laughed and said, "You made it by a nickel." I said, "You have no idea." I left the van there and walked to a park not far away. I sat there and prayed, "What next God?" I had four days to get from Sioux Falls, South Dakota to Window Rock, Arizona on the New Mexico and Arizona border. A pastor friend had asked me months before if I would do praise and worship on the Navajo Reservation there for some of the Native Americans and I had told him that I would be there. I had talked to him a few times over the past month and he was aware of my journey and the challenges that I had endured and he was praying that I still could make it to the camp. After a few hours I walked back to the tire store and the manager said that the van was ready. He told me in all his years in the business, he had never seen a tire like that still hold together. He asked, "How many miles did you drive with your tire like that?" I answered that I had made it over three thousand miles. He shook his head and said, "There is somebody is watching over you." I smiled and told him, "There is."

I had a long way to go, so I got back on the road. I had a full tank of gas, a little food and a new tire. My goal was to make it back to IHOP in Kansas City. After I had been driving for a few hours, the Lord began to tell me that He was going to start picking up the pace with those people and ministries that had humbled themselves and had laid themselves out before Him in brokenness and humility. He was now going to pick up the pace. It was still going to be at His speed, but in our speed and in the natural, the doors were going to start opening for those who had been faithful and had gone through the trials and tribulations and had endured the test. Now doors were going to be open quickly and they were going to go through them. He was going to start moving us physically faster through different doors and He showed me a picture of soldiers training like in a Marine boot camp, all running at a certain speed. They started out slow, then the sergeant yelled out orders and they picked up the pace. Then the soldiers heard the order for double-time and they began taking off.

The Lord said that this was what He was doing with His servants. He would be picking up the pace with those who had humbled themselves before Him and He would bring favor to their lives. Then He showed me two boats in a river. One was a small motorboat kind of putting along which represented the people and the ministries that hadn't bent their knees and humbled themselves before God. All of a sudden big powerboats were racing by them on the same journey, and a huge wave of water from the bigger boats almost overtook and swamped the small motorboat. The Lord explained that the large powerboats were those who had stayed humble and broken for Him. They were the ones that were going to do great and mighty things and do them quickly because time was becoming short.

42

GIVING BACK

~

As I continued on my way to the International House of Prayer in Kansas City, the Lord was talking to me about IHOP. They were coming up on seven years of 24/7 prayer and worship and the Lord told me that seven years was a sign of completion. I didn't have any idea when exactly IHOP had started, so when I arrived there again I picked up a flyer that had information about when they opened. I scanned the paper and found the date: September 19, 1999. So, September 19th it would be seven years and I was there Monday, September 4th. I thought, "Wow! It's almost seven years." The Lord spoke to me that we needed to have seven days of fasting, prayer, and repentance to help bring in the revival many people were praying for. So I asked the Lord, "Do You want me to tell someone about seven days of fasting, prayer, and repentance?" I didn't get an answer, so I went inside. I had just been there eleven days before and coming back almost felt like being in a dream. Was I really here again and how long was the Lord going to keep me here this time? Or was I just supposed to bring a message and then be off on the next part of this journey?

As I entered the worship sanctuary, I noticed it was full. It seemed IHOP was having a meeting with the staff and the students. They were discussing an upcoming conference on spiritual warfare that was to be held that weekend. As I waited, a thought came to me, "I wonder if my friends from Norway are in this room." They were students there, so they were probably around somewhere. So I looked around and spotted the husband with two of his sons just a few rows ahead of me. I thought, "Maybe he's the one that I'm supposed to bring this message to." I kept an eye on him and when his sons started to get a little restless and they got up to walk out of the sanctuary, I followed them. When we made it out into the hallway I said hello and they were happy to see me. The father said, "You are back." I told him that the Lord had had me stop on my way back to Arizona. He asked me, "Why did the Lord have you stop here?" I told him what the Lord had said about the seven days of fasting, praying, and repenting. I told him that I thought I was to share this with him and that the Lord would tell him what to do next. He said he would pray and ask the Lord what to do about the message. He said, "Bobby, will we ever see you again?" I told him that I was sure God would make a way. I said that I was excited to see what the Lord was going to do with them, as a family, for their obedience in leaving Norway and coming to IHOP. I asked him, "Do you know yet if you will stay in the United States or go back to Norway when you graduate from the school?" He told me he didn't know. He said, "I hope that we can meet again." I told him we would. I said, "I have to go now. I have a lot of miles to drive today. I will pray for you and your family." With that I got into my van and started driving across Kansas.

I got as far as Salina by 3:00 P.M. Well, I was in the middle of Kansas. *Now what Lord?* So, as always, I hung out at a Walmart, a grocery store, a Costco, and asked the Lord, "Who am I waiting for?" I was sitting outside of Walmart when a young lady that worked at the nail salon inside sat next to me. She was on break. She looked at me and said, "Do you mind if I smoke?" I told her no, not at all. I asked her how her day was going. She said it wasn't too bad. She asked me, "So, are you from Salina?" I said no, I was on a journey across America and was on my way back to Arizona. She talked to me about this small town and how there wasn't much to do. She had grown up here and as she talked about her life I could tell that she didn't have much hope for a better tomorrow. She was a single mom with two children. I told her that I was a Christian and that God had made a way for me so many times when I had thought there was none. I gave her my card and told her that I would pray for her. She said, "Thank you, I have to get back to work." I spent the rest of the evening just hanging out in front of Walmart. It was almost 9:30 P.M. when I parked my van on the outer edge of Walmart's parking lot with the other RVs and trailers. I tried to get some rest but, as usual, I wasn't able to get much while sitting straight up in the driver's seat of my van. I woke up the next day and drove around town with the little gas I had left, praying and hanging out at the various stores and parks. I prayed all day and waited for a phone call from someone, anyone, to help me get down the road. I spotted a few pawnshops, but again the Lord wasn't going to let me pawn any of my DJ gear to get me where I needed to go. I thought, "Lord, you have had me haul all of this gear all over the country, why?" I heard the Lord say, "I want you to be ready to play or help someone at a moment's notice." I said, "Okay, Lord." I spent the rest of the afternoon sitting in front of a grocery store and then went back to Walmart to camp for the night. It was Tuesday, September 5th, and I had three days to make it to Window Rock, Arizona.

At about 10:00 P.M. a large RV towing a trailer with a motorcycle was pulling into the parking lot. As I watched him pull in, the driver ran over the curb with his trailer and motorcycle on back. I jumped out of my van and ran over to help him. He got out of the RV. He was stuck and I told him I would help guide him to get his trailer off the curb. He had turned the RV too sharp and would need to back up carefully. Well, with a little help, he got off the curb. He had put a nice dent in his RV from turning too sharply, but we both agreed it could have been worse. He thanked me for my help. He said his name was Charlie and his wife's name was Sandy and they had a little dog that looked just like Dorothy's dog from the movie The Wizard of Oz. I thought, "Wait a minute, I'm in Kansas, if this dog's name is Toto, I better go back to my van because I'm dreaming." I asked them, "Your dog's name isn't Toto, is it?" They both laughed and said no. Charlie said, "We are going to stay here for the night. Do you want to have dinner with us?" I hadn't had much to eat in the past few days, so I gladly accepted their invitation. Sandy mentioned, "I have to go into Walmart and get a few things. Why don't the both of you wait for me in the RV? I'll be right back." She came back shortly and made a great meal for all of us. We ended up talking for a couple of hours. They asked me about my journey and what had brought me to the Walmart parking lot in Salina, Kansas. I asked them where they were from and they told me Boise, Idaho. They had driven the RV all the way to Tulsa, Oklahoma to buy the motorcycle that was on the trailer. I asked Charlie, "Why did you have to travel so far to get the motorcycle?" He said that he had been looking for a motorcycle that was the same year and make of the one he had had when he was in college many years ago. He wanted to restore the bike as a project at home. He was retired and his wife was planning to retire that year. They had just bought the RV. It was only a couple of years old and this was the first time they had had a chance to use it. He laughed and said he was going to have to get a little better around those parking lot corners. They asked me if I was going to be around in the morning and I told them I would. They asked me to join them for breakfast and coffee. I told them I would and headed back to my van.

The next morning I was up early reading my bible with the hatch door open while sitting on the bumper, when Charlie walked up to say good morning. He looked into the van and noticed all the gear. It was totally packed up to the ceiling. He walked up to my driver's side door and looked at everything on the passenger's side also packed to the ceiling. He said, "How do you see your passenger's side mirror?" I said, "I can see through an open area I made through all the gear and I use my side mirror also." He said, "Bobby, how do you sleep with all this packed in here?" I told him, "I sleep sitting straight up like I'm driving." A sad look came over his face and he said, "I'm sorry, I didn't know. You should have slept in the fold out couch in the RV." I said, "Charlie, it's okay. I have been sleeping like this for weeks. It's been hard on my back, but I will make it." He said, "Come on up to the RV. Let's have some breakfast." I brought my portfolio of pictures of my stone designs and the ministry picture book of events that I had done for the youth. Both Charlie and Sandy were excited to see all the stone designs and ministry events for the youth. I gave them my card and we talked and laughed some more and then Charlie said, "Bobby, I need you to get in your van and drive across the street. I'm going to fill up your van." So I drove over to the gas station and Charlie filled up the van with gas and handed me twenty dollars and said, "This is for a hamburger, and with the gas you have, you'll make it to Denver, right?" I told him I would. I asked Charlie if I could pray for him and he said, "Yes." So here we were praying at a gas station. I knew people were watching but I didn't care. I prayed for Charlie and his wife, that the Lord would bless them and that they would enjoy life. Charlie's eyes started to water up. I gave him a hug and thanked him again. He told me that they would also be going through Denver and would keep an eye out for me along the road in case I needed help. I thanked him again and got into the van and headed off. I needed to get to Denver by that afternoon.

As I tracked though Kansas, I was thinking of all the people that the Lord had brought to me along this journey and how our paths had crossed by His timing and how He was teaching me to wait and hear His voice. He was also teaching me that everyday was about learning to die to myself and to my will. I thought of all the places I had been the past few months and all the ways the Lord had used me. All of it was for Him and not about me. I wasn't sure how and when He was going to heal my marriage and my children, I just knew He would do what He said He would do for me and my family as I was faithful to go and do what He was asking me to.

I was on the road somewhere in the middle of Kansas when I saw a sign for McDonald's and pulled off the freeway to get a hamburger. As I pulled into the parking lot, I saw a guy in his early twenties with a backpack and a dog on a chain. They were in a grassy area off the parking lot. He was getting his dog some water. As I parked the van I heard the Lord say, "Make sure you get him some food to eat." He had a walk-man with his headset on and wore his hair in a ponytail. He looked like he had been on the road for a while. I went inside McDonald's and stood in line to order my food. The place was very busy. It had to be the only one for many miles because it was so packed. I had ordered my food and stepped back to wait for my order when the man behind me almost ran me over to get to the register. He was a businessman in a three-piece suit. While he was putting his order in, the guy from outside with the dog stepped up right behind the businessman. He was looking at the dollar menu while counting his dimes, nickels and pennies. He took off his headphones and started counting his money with the music in his headset still playing loudly. Hearing the music, the businessman turned around and looked at him in disgust. The businessman never left the counter; he just stood there like his order was more important than those before him. The lady behind the counter said, "Could you step aside so I can take this man's order?" The guy with the headset walked up to the counter still counting his money. The lady said, "You look about as broke as I am." He ordered a hamburger and small fries and gave the lady at the counter all of his change. I watched as the businessman just looked him up and down. It was obvious the kid had been using drugs. His face and arms had pockmarks and there were tracks on his arms. I had seen this so many times working with the homeless and drug-addicted people in Phoenix who had been using crystal meth and heroin. When my food came up, I asked the businessman to move so I could get my order. I took my food, turned around to the man with the headset and handed him five dollars and said, "This is for your next meal." He smiled and said, "God bless you." The businessman was watching and when I stepped away, the businessman was left with everyone in the restaurant staring at him. They had all put down their food and were watching what was going on between myself, the businessman and the man with the ponytail and headset. I had been in that position. Every time I had found myself judging someone, God would put it right back in my lap like He did to that businessman. I was still learning how to love God and help people and not judge. I had a long way to go if I was going to be like Jesus, but wasn't that what the journey was all about? I was thankful for the money Charlie had given me earlier and I had taken some of the seed he had planted in me and planted it in that young man in the way of a meal. I had always done this.

I got back on the road and headed for Denver to see my sister-in-law and then I would be on my way to Window Rock. I got to Denver in the late afternoon and spent a few hours at my sister-in-law's home and she helped me with gas for the van. It would have been great to sleep on the couch or a bed, but I didn't have any time left. There were still a lot of miles to make up on the road, so I had to go. When I made it just past Colorado Springs, I found a rest stop to sleep at. I was totally exhausted. The next morning I got up and drove until Grants, New Mexico, eighty miles from Window Rock. I couldn't get any further as I was out of gas and out of money. I called my pastor friend and told him where I was. He told me he would wire me some money so I could make it to the camp. I got the money, put some gas in the van, and drove to Gallup, New Mexico to spend the night in another Walmart parking lot. It was raining so hard I could barely see to drive, but I made it.

43

WE ARE ALL THE SAME

~

I got up the next morning, Friday, September 8th. I had all afternoon to drive to the camp in Window Rock, the capital of the Navajo Nation. When I got into town, they were having a huge rodeo and fair and there were thousands of people just camped along the sidewalk and anywhere they could park. The camp was just outside of town. I was told I was going to have to travel a long way on a dirt road to get there. It was really crazy to see all the gang graffiti everywhere on the reservation. Drugs and alcohol were also everywhere. The reservation was one of the most beautiful places I had ever seen, yet the people who live there have some of the most difficult challenges facing their culture and their youth. That was why we were asked to come and minister to some of the young people on the reservation. I got to the turn off for the camp. The mountains around me were incredible. I was praying that my van would make it on these dirt roads. It was so loaded with gear that I was sitting just a few inches off the ground. The area had gotten a lot of rain over the past few days so I was hoping the roads were dry and that there were not too many ruts.

It seemed like I could only drive a mile at a time. I kept stopping to take pictures of the mountains and surrounding valleys. It was more beautiful than anything I had ever seen. I traveled about fifteen miles down the dirt road, scraping the bottom of my van quite a few times. I finally made it to the camp. It was straight down a road that dropped into the camp area. The camp was in a large bowl shaped area with trees and mountains surrounding it. I was the first one there. I got out of the van and walked over to this stream only to be surprised by two deer getting a drink. About half an hour later, everyone started to show up. It was great to see some of my friends and a few pastors that I knew. I got to meet a group of young people from a church that had come to minister with us. I set up my DJ equipment in the dining hall. It was shaped like a large A-frame cabin. My pastor friend was going to do worship and then I would play and do worship after him. More people arrived around dinnertime and a group of Navajo young people arrived around 6:00 P.M. They were older than I thought they were going to be, ranging between eighteen and twenty-three years old. We all greeted each other and said hello. My pastor friends had been coming up to the Reservation for five years and knew the other pastors from the area. After dinner we started in with praise and worship and my friend led the way. I would play the sound tracks to the songs he wanted and he and his son would sing along. It was a powerful time. After he was done, I just kept going with the music I had. All of a sudden a few of our Navajo friends came from the back of the dining hall and stood with the others, their arms lifted to the Lord. I noticed this one young lady was crying as I was playing the worship music. Just then the Lord showed me a vision of her. It was one of the most powerful and real visions that I had ever had about anyone. I just kept playing music for another forty-five minutes and then some people got up to share the Word and talk about some of the things we would be doing over the next few days. I couldn't get the vision out of my mind and went to sleep that night still thinking about what I had seen.

The next morning I shared the vision with my pastor friend. He said that when the pastor from the Reservation arrived that morning he would have me share it with him. I hadn't had the opportunity to meet that pastor the night before because he had been called away on urgent matters and would not be arriving until later that morning. When he arrived a little later on we were introduced. He was a pastor that had been on the reservation for many years and had built a strong bond and trust with the Navajo people. He had also handpicked the young people to be with us that weekend. I shared with him what had happened the night before during worship and told him about the vision I had seen about this young lady. As I explained, he started to cry and said, "Bobby, you have no idea the things that have surrounded her life this past year. I have been praying that the Lord would visit her and change her life." We were in the dining hall while everyone else was having free time outside. The girl was in the back sitting at a table by her self near one of the windows, reading the Bible. The pastor asked me if I would share the vision with her, if she wanted me to. I told him I would. He walked over to her table, talked to her for a few minutes and then motioned me to come over and sit down beside him across from the girl. I began to share, "Last night during worship, the Lord showed me something about you. When I was playing worship music you came forward and stood there for a while and then you lifted your hands to worship. The Lord showed me that you were standing in this campground where we are now, but you were out in the middle of a field of dead weeds with the trees all around on the mountains, except they were black and gray. Even the sky above you was black and gray. Everything was dead and then you lifted your arms to heaven and I saw the trees shake and tremble, like an earthquake, and the ground shook and there was this tremendous sound that got louder and louder. You had your arms lifted to heaven and all of a sudden a wind that I can't describe came from one end of the mountains and roared right through you and your hair was blown straight back and in a second everything turned to color and became alive. The sky cleared, the sun came out and the field and the surrounding area became full of flowers of every color." I explained that my words could not describe what the Lord had shown me. I looked at her and tears were coming down her face. She told me that when I had started playing worship music that night she had been in the back of the dining hall and felt like she was supposed to come up to the front where I was. She had never had that feeling before. When she came up front, she said she felt her arms go up and Jesus appeared to her and asked if He could come into her life and be her Savior. She said that when she replied yes, He had shown her the exact same vision that I had described to her. She explained that darkness had been around her for a long time, but now she was free to live again. I just sat there and smiled. Later, when the pastor told me the events and situations that had surrounded her life over the past year and his prayers for her, I was blown away. God is so good. To be a part of this was beyond words, and to see her set free was more amazing than I could explain.

The next few days were full of fun and excitement as we built relationships and overcame walls in our own lives together. On the last morning of our camp, the pastor asked us to form a big circle and hold hands. He asked us to state our names and share something we had learned while we were at camp. When it came to be my turn I introduced myself like this: "My name is Bobby Dendy. I am a Servant of the Lord, a Warrior for Christ and a Follower of Jesus." It just came out of my mouth. I couldn't stop it. I think it was defining just who I was. More and more as this journey continued to unfold, it had been defining who I was in Christ. I told the group that morning as we all stood in a circle that what I had learned at camp was that the Navajo people were a proud people and a good people who had endured much pain and suffering, just as we all do. We all need a Savior to bring healing, hope, and restoration into our lives and our families. As I looked at their faces around the circle, they smiled and nodded in agreement. I thought of the poem *Happytown*. It didn't matter if you were from Window Rock or from New York; we were all the same. We all said goodbye and packed up for the journey home, except I didn't have a home to go to... at least not yet.

44
ONE PLACE

~

It was Sunday, September 10th. I had been gone from my family for over two months and I knew there were a million unanswered questions as to why and where I had gone, what had been the purpose of this journey, and was God really in the middle of all of it or was I just on some crazy pilgrimage to fulfill my own dream. Well, I was never on vacation. I was on an assignment. And if you could see all the tears I had cried over my family that would be obvious. As I left the camp that day I was reflecting back on all the people I had met over the past months on my 'Journey for the King.' I was thinking about the way I would get to know these people from all over the country, build a friendship and a common bond, share together our love for Jesus, just to have to leave them and move on. It was way too hard. Many of my new friends had asked if I could stay longer and when I would be back with my family. I kept thinking about the disciples with Jesus. How difficult that must have been to travel with Him, fellowship with believers, share the Love of Christ making new converts, and to share their love and passion for people and then leave. It was like being torn from your family, and I knew a little something about that after the journey I had been on.

It had been months since I left my broken trailer at the youth camp in Payson, AZ. I prayed, "Lord, I need that trailer to do more events that people have asked me to be a part of." When I had returned to Phoenix, I shared the story of my broken trailer with my friend Shad Ciampi. He looked at me and said, "Let's go get it." Shad is a very gifted welder, mechanic, you name it, so I drove with him in his truck from Phoenix to Payson, 100 miles away, to fix the trailer and bring it back. I had a great time with my friend that day. We laughed a lot. Shad said that he and his family would pray for my family and me. I had really needed something to encourage me to continue on, and with Shad's help I got that answer from God. I went back to Cottonwood, Arizona to stay with Pastor Greg and his family. I called my wife and, after being gone for so long and still having no answers as to why I wasn't back in Phoenix with a job, she didn't even want to talk to me.

Over the next few months I occasionally visited my wife and children. I still wasn't allowed to stay at the house, but at least I could visit. I would then drive back to Cottonwood and sleep on Pastor Greg's couch or another friend's couch. When the holidays came around I got work doing some corporate parties and I was able to be with my wife and children that Christmas. The New Year was coming and I was still living out of my van and staying in Cottonwood. The Lord was telling me that Cottonwood was going to be my home, but I didn't want to live in Cottonwood. I wanted to live in Colorado or Coeur d'Alene, Idaho. I knew that Phoenix was no longer going to be home. I knew the Lord would heal my marriage and my family. I just wanted to get on with it. I was still getting requests to do events for ministries and help them and I did. My wife wanted me to get a full-time job in Phoenix, but I could not take being in Phoenix. It wasn't the city itself. God was doing something in me and He wouldn't let me go. I didn't want to live in Cottonwood and I kept telling the Lord so, but that was getting me nowhere fast. God started to give me a love for Cottonwood and the surrounding areas. So, after eight months of being away from my family, I asked the Lord, "Please, can we all be in one place as a family?"

45

GOD IS GOOD

~

The Lord spoke to me on April 10th. He said to ask Pastor Frank of Emmanuel Fellowship if he would allow me to play praise and worship at their church 24/7 for seven days. I had only spoken to Pastor Frank a few times and said to the Lord, "He doesn't even know me." The Lord said to me, **"Ask him."**

I was thinking to myself, "After all I have been through, if the Lord wants me to do this for only seven days; that is ok with me." As I was praying, the Lord told me, "If the emergency rooms of a hospital are open twenty four hours a day, seven days a week, then why isn't my house open like that?" When I went to see Pastor Frank later that day, I shared with him what the Lord had told me and I asked him if I could do praise and worship in the sanctuary for seven days and nights. I told him that I would bring in my own sound system and would work around their worship and service times. I explained to him about the many years I had been doing this at other churches, camps, and outreach events and shared with him the miracles that occurred as we lifted the name of Jesus through praise and worship. As we saturated the area where we were with worship and the Word, God did amazing things. I told Pastor Frank that I would leave my sound system in the church over night and leave the CDs on repeat so that the music would play until I got there in the morning.

Pastor Frank agreed that he thought worship 24/7 in the sanctuary was a good idea. They also had someone who came early every morning to clean, so there would be someone to open the doors. He asked if I would like to set up on the stage. I told him that I would rather set up at the front of the stage on the floor in the corner, not on the main stage. I could set up behind some chairs and put my speakers on stage. I asked him not to tell people, other than the church staff, what was going on. I said that the Lord would do what He wanted to do if we didn't hype up or promote what was going on. Pastor Frank agreed.

So, on Wednesday, April 11th, at 10:45 A.M., I started playing praise and worship music in the sanctuary of Emmanuel Fellowship. Over the span of sixteen years I had recorded somewhere around fifteen nonstop praise and worship CDs. Wherever I went, as I ministered to young people and those that were hungry for the presence of God, the CDs would run. They ran anywhere from sixty to seventy five minutes long. I also have hundreds of worship CDs by various artists that I can play at anytime. I asked the Lord what He wanted me to play at Emmanuel. The Lord had me play Praise CD number four. This CD, along with many others, was recorded in a small barn as I was ministering to young people from a group home that my friend ran in Phoenix. I just numbered them as the Lord led me to record them. It was only a few years earlier that the Lord began to give me a title for the CD before He gave me the songs to add. All of the numbered CDs had a strong theme and anointing that the Lord had put on each of them. I had given away thousands of these, each with its own message. Praise CD number four was about the Love and Forgiveness of God.

The first day at Emmanuel, the Lord had me play it for the whole day and leave it on until the next morning. I was staying at Pastor Greg's house and left his house early to get to the church. Pastor Greg was working and living, with his wife Debbie, at a Christian Retreat Center in Cornville, which was about five miles away from the church. When I arrived at the church I saw Pastor Frank. He asked me if I needed anything and I told him that I was fine. I continued playing the same CD and a few people came in that morning to simply sit in the presence of the Lord.

Around 11:15 A.M. on Thursday, April 12th, I watched as a teenager walked down to the front of the sanctuary and sat down for about a half hour. He eventually got up, looked in my direction and left the sanctuary. Twenty minutes later, the youth pastor for Emmanuel Fellowship came up to the DJ booth that I had made in the corner and said, "Bobby, did you see the young man that was just in here?" I said, "Yes, why?" The youth pastor replied, "Well, he goes to the high school a few blocks from here. He had an open hour before his lunch and was at the high school when he heard the Lord say to him, "Go to the church." He told me he couldn't understand why he needed to go to the church since there was nothing going on there during the day. Why would God tell him to go? But he walked here anyway and when he opened the front doors, he heard the music playing in the sanctuary and the Lord told him to go inside and sit down. So he came inside and sat down to listen and the Lord told him he was going to be an armor bearer, so he came to my office to ask me what that meant." The youth pastor told me how excited he was to have me at the church. I just smiled and told him that it was great to be here. It was just a little over twenty-four hours and the Lord was already speaking to people. I knew when I first met Pastor Frank and Pastor Juan, the worship leader there, that this was a church and pastoral staff that was hungry for revival and maybe I was going to be a small part of it.

The rest of the day and into the early evening, the Lord had me play praise and worship CD six. This CD is a very deep CD that is asking and petitioning God for healing and revival. One of the praise and worship teams came into the sanctuary around 6:00 P.M. to rehearse for Sunday. As the musicians came in, they gave me curious stares, wondering what was going on. I just smiled and kept playing. Pastor Juan told me to keep playing until he gave me the sign to drop the music level down. One of the musicians that played the guitar came up to me and introduced himself. He asked about what I was doing and I told him I would be playing praise and worship in the sanctuary for the next six days, around rehearsal and service times. He explained that he had been attending Emmanuel for the past few years and he had never experienced this. When he had pulled into the parking lot that night, he could feel the presence of God even in his car outside. I just smiled and said, "It's great isn't it." He said, "Thanks for being here", and he went to set up for rehearsal. The band and Pastor Juan were really good. I was enjoying their worship. When they were finished, I put the volume back up on the CD and left for Pastor Greg's house. Pastor Juan said he would lock up the church and see me in the morning.

Once again I arrived early and the Lord said to keep playing praise and worship CD number six. I said, "Lord, why?" He told me His children were in need of deep healing and that would only happened in His presence. So I just kept playing that CD that morning. Some of the church staff came into the sanctuary and started to cry. A few other members of the church also showed up throughout the morning and, as the music played, I watched them come to alter crying and weeping, just a few feet away from me. It was right before lunchtime when the doors of the sanctuary opened once again and I saw a woman come in. I couldn't make out what she was wearing or see her face because she was too far away, but as she sat down, I could hear her crying. She had been weeping for a long time when one of the ladies at the altar got up and went to where she was sitting and hugged her and cried with her. Later, after the lady left, the lady that was praying at the altar came up to tell me her story. She said, "Did you see that woman I was praying for?" I said, "Yes," but she was a ways away from me and didn't hear me. She went on, "Well, she is a motorcycle rider. She had been riding her motorcycle by the church when something pulled her into this parking lot and told her to come inside. She has never been here before and never wanted to set foot in a church again. She told me that she had been hurt badly by the church and wanted nothing to do with it. She said she wasn't sure she could ever go back to God's house but when she came into the sanctuary here she was able to sit in His presence like this." I just smiled and said, "God is good."

46

CURSES & BLESSINGS

~

It hadn't even been two full days and the Lord was already calling and healing people in His presence. I continued to play the same CD and came back again to the church Saturday morning. I was in the sanctuary by myself until about 8:00 A.M. when the church intercessors and prayer group came in. They all went straight to the altar and onto their faces on the carpet. I never said a thing to them. As I continued to play the music, I thought, "This is the church I have been waiting for." Seeing the prayer team at the church just go to the altar to seek the Lord, I knew I was in the right place. After about twenty minutes they asked me to bring the music down and inquired about how I had come to Emmanuel Fellowship. I shared with them some of the Journey that had brought me to their door and the need for healing in my marriage, my family and my own life. It was so refreshing and encouraging meeting the prayer warriors of this church. The rest of the day and into the evening I continued to play CDs number four and six. It had now been three days and the Lord would not let me play anything else. It was obvious to me that this house was to be a place of healing.

When Sunday morning came around, I was curious to see how the congregation would react to my being there. The church had two morning services, one at 8:00 A.M. and another at 10:15 A.M. The 8:00 A.M. service was more of a traditional service for the older people in the church and there were about 80 people in attendance that morning. Again I had my curious stares and a few people came up to me to welcome me to their church. I enjoyed the hymns and the music they played that morning and I was really able to see the diversity of Pastor Juan and the worship band. As Pastor Frank preached, he stuck to our agreement and did not introduce me or say anything about me to the congregation. Again, after the service a few people came to say hello and thanked me for playing music before the service. I was still playing music as the worship team and band came in to practice for the second service. The church had three praise and worship bands for the different services so I met some more members of the worship team. Some of the musicians came over to say hello and asked about my being there and how long I would be at the church and I answered that, at that point, I would only be there for a few more days.

The second service offered a contemporary style of praise and worship with a small choir. They were really good and I thought, "Lord, the worship teams and the bands that are at this church could play at any church in the country, large or small." I had come from a church of five thousand people and the talents and gifts in this church were just as good or better than many I had seen and been a part of. As the church started to fill up for the second service, there were many more curious stares. A few young people came over to say hi and ask questions. Again, as in the first service, Pastor Frank did not mention me, or what I was doing there. I had been told that the church held a little over four hundred people and it was packed in the second service. There was a real hunger for God in the house that morning. Before they took up the offering that morning, the same as in the first service, Pastor Juan prayed for the seven thousand souls that would be saved and added to the churches in the Verde Valley that preached the Gospel of Jesus Christ. He also prayed that the churches would be overflowing with the presence of God. I once again thought, "I'm in the right place. Not only are they praying for their own church, but for all the churches that preach the Gospel to be blessed." When the service was over, many more people came over to say hi and ask how long I would be staying at Emmanuel.

I continued to play music all afternoon until the 6:00 P.M. Sunday night service. Again, the worship and word from Pastor Frank were great. I left the church that night and told everyone I would be back early Monday morning. I had talked to my wife on Saturday and had told her what was going on and that the seven days the Lord had asked me to do was going to end on the upcoming Wednesday, the 18th of April. My wife had asked me if I then planned on coming to Phoenix and I told her I would return as soon as my assignment from the Lord was finished in Cottonwood.

It was now Monday morning and the presence of the Lord was much stronger than any of the previous days. The Lord was still not letting me play any CDs other than the ones I had already been playing. Throughout the day and into the evening, a few people came into the sanctuary to sit in the presence of the Lord, mostly women. Almost everyone who came in would cry. The Lord was simply asking me to bathe the sanctuary with worship. I was not concerned with how many people would show up. The Lord would bring who He wanted, when He wanted to. I was just doing my part to worship and to seek breakthrough from the Lord; for my family, myself, the church and the community I was now in. When I drove back to Pastor Greg's house that night, I thought, "Only two days left to go." The next morning I was on my way to the sanctuary. I had just crossed the bridge about one mile from the church when the presence of the Lord filled my van. I started to cry so hard that I could hardly control my van and I could barely see to drive. I made it into the church parking lot, turned off the van and just sat there crying. The Lord was showing me what was coming to Emmanuel Fellowship and the Verde Valley. I saw thousands and thousands of cars driving into the Verde Valley from every direction. The whole city of Cottonwood was on fire for the Lord. People were getting saved everywhere. People were praying for other people at the gas stations, at the store, at the high school, at restaurants and the park. I saw thousands of people gathering there. They were camped in the parking lot and any place they could park in campers with tents, RVs, and buses. There were thousands of young people from all over the country. Churches all over the Verde Valley were overflowing with people from everywhere. It was such a beautiful and awe-inspiring vision and it overwhelmed my heart.

Just then, Rachel, the church secretary, pulled into the parking lot. I had my window down on the van and waved to her to come over. When she got to my door, she asked, "Are you alright?" I said, "Give me your hand" and I started to speak a prophesy over the church, the Verde Valley, and over Rachel. It was so strong. I still had my seatbelt on and could not move. The power of God was so strong that I could hardly stand it. Rachel asked, "Are you going to be okay?" I told her that I would be okay and she left to go into the church to open up the office. Shortly after, I saw Pastor Frank arrive and walk into the church. I couldn't talk and I couldn't move. I just sat in the van for a half hour and prayed. Finally the Lord let me get out of the van, but I could hardly walk. The Lord said to go into the church and tell Pastor Frank that I had a word for him. As I walked into the office, Rachel asked me again, "Are you okay?" I said, "Yes. Can I speak to Pastor Frank?" She went into his office and then came back out to tell me that he would see me. I asked Rachel to come into the office also. I always like to have a witness to the words I give if that is possible. I told Pastor Frank about the events of that morning that led up to being in his office. I told him what the Lord had showed me about Emmanuel Fellowship. Then the power of God hit me again. As I was speaking, the Lord had me ask Pastor Frank, "Do you really want this revival?" Then the Lord asked me to ask him the same question again. At this time, I thought I was going to explode. Then the Lord told me to ask him another question. Even as I was asking the question, I thought in my mind, "Wow! This is a hard question to answer." I asked Pastor Frank the question the Lord told me to ask. "Are you willing to allow those who have cursed you to come to this house to be healed?" Pastor Frank's eyes got really large and I was weeping so hard that I could barely ask him the same question again, but I did. It didn't seem physically possible, but his eyes got even bigger still. Finally, I asked the question one more time and Pastor Frank replied, "Yes." He would allow those who had cursed him to come to Emmanuel to be healed. Then the Lord had me tell Pastor Frank that he was well able to handle what was coming next and not to fear. The Lord was also going to send him help. When I was done with what the Lord had me say, I thought, "Wow! That was a very intense question. How many of us today would allow someone who had cursed us to receive forgiveness and healing, even if it is what the Lord asks of us."

47

IT'S OKAY WITH ME

~

It was day six of the seven days that the Lord asked me to stay at Emmanuel. I was still not allowed to change the CDs that I was playing. CD number four and CD number six played throughout the afternoon and into the evening. It was early evening when Pastor Frank came to talk to me. He said, "Bobby, if you feel that the Lord wants you to stay longer, it is okay with me." I told Pastor Frank that the Lord had not asked me to stay longer, but if He did, I would let him know. That night as I drove to Pastor Greg's house, I asked the Lord, "Why am I still only playing these two CDs?" The Lord responded, "The healing is not just for this house, but for others that would come."

I arrived early Wednesday morning, day seven. As I was playing music, the Lord told me to ask Pastor Frank for twenty-one more days. I said, "Lord, I want to get back to my family and sleep in my own bed." The Lord said, "You are to sleep in this house and keep the doors open 24/7 for those who need to come in at anytime, day or night." I said, "Okay, Lord. I will ask Pastor Frank for twenty-one days more and tell him about sleeping in the church and keeping the doors open through the night." So, when I saw Pastor Frank that morning I told him what the Lord had told me to say and he responded, "Let's go twenty-one more days." He continued, "We should let the congregation know that the church will be open 24/7 and explain to them what you are doing here." I agreed, so that night he told the Wednesday night service what was happening and that worship music would be in the sanctuary 24/7 for the next twenty-one days. Pastor Frank had tried to put me in a nice hotel for the first seven days that I was at Emmanuel. I thanked him for his generosity, but chose to stay with Pastor Greg. It was what the Lord wanted me to do. And now, for the next three weeks, it was going to be my sleeping bag and me on the floor of the church. I had an old calendar that I had picked up at a grocery store and I marked down the next twenty-one days.

As I thought about sleeping on the floor, I remembered a church that I played worship music at in Tulare, California that was having a revival. It was a small church that was playing recorded worship music in their sanctuary 24/7. This had been about three years before. A friend of mine in Phoenix, who was a worship leader and involved with the Promise Keepers, had told me about this church. He explained that he had many pastoral friends in California, from up and down the coast, who were going to this church. They were telling him that the presence of God was so strong that they could barely make it through the door. My friend said, "Bobby, you have to go there and play at that church." I told him, "It's about ten hours away." He said, "So? You still have to go." I went the next week. I played at the church and experienced the amazing things God was doing there. People from all over America and Canada were coming to this church. They provided pillows and blankets for those who wanted to stay in the church through the night although the doors were locked at 10:00 P.M. because of the neighborhood. When the sun came up each morning, the pastor would unlock the front door of the church for people to come in. There was also a side door that they kept open for anyone who was in the church that might need to leave before morning. If you were in the church, you could sleep on the pews or the floor. There was a house right next door that had been converted to feed people. They had showers there and a food bank. I met people that God had brought from all over the country for healing and many other reasons.

I had an opportunity to speak with and pray with some men from the Dream Center in Los Angeles. Every weekend one of the leaders from the street team there would bring a few men to this church to experience the presence of the Lord. Some people, both men and women, had been there for months and had come to help the church with their feeding programs. Others came to pray and help in whatever way they could. The stories of how they had heard about this church blew me away. One story in particular involved an older couple from Canada who were in their early seventies. They had spent all the money they had on cancer treatments for the wife. She was in a lot of pain and getting no relief. They had sold their home and moved into a small trailer. They were very desperate. One night, they were at a small bible study when the Lord spoke to the wife and said, "Tulare, California." They didn't know were that was, so they looked on a map of the U.S.A. and eventually found it. They drove all the way to Tulare and started to ask around for a church in town that was having revival. They were directed to the church that I spoke about. I listened as they told me about the testimony of their journey to the church in Tulare. When they arrived the first day, nothing happened to either one of them, but on the third day, the wife was totally healed. All the pain was gone! She was dancing around. When she told this part of the story, I could see the joy of the Lord all over her face. She told how simply sitting in the presence of the Lord and reading her Bible there at the church had set her totally free from cancer. She and her husband had now been at the church for over two weeks. I may write about my two personal experiences at this church someday.

48

BETWEEN THEM AND GOD

~

I know the Lord was having me reflect on my experiences at that church because of some of the things that were coming to Emmanuel Fellowship and the Verde Valley. I had called my wife back in Phoenix to tell her that I was going to be in Cottonwood for another twenty-one days at the church. Again her question was why wasn't I coming back to Phoenix to get a job and work on our marriage, what little was left of it. I told her, "It is twenty-one days that the Lord has asked me for and the Lord said He would take care of us. He also said that there are people He wants to heal in this church and in the surrounding areas." When my wife hung up the phone, I thought to myself, "I'm only ninety miles from home, but I feel so far away from the healing that I desperately need for my family." I then thought of one of my friend's comments to me. He said he believed that God was going to heal my family and me on this journey. I knew deep down that God was already doing this even if I didn't see any evidence on the surface. God has always been faithful even when I was not. I knew that whatever the Lord was doing, it was on a huge scale. He was doing something never seen before, by me or anyone else.

It was now the eighth day at Emmanuel Fellowship and the Lord allowed me to add CD number ten to the mix. Now I was rotating three CD's. Sometimes I would play one for eight hours and the next for one hour. The Lord directed me to change the music according to how He wanted it and I was always amazed that when I changed a CD, someone new would walk into the sanctuary. Every morning I would wake up around 5:30 A.M. and pray over every chair in the sanctuary, over four hundred of them. I would pray that the Lord would bring healing and deliverance to those who sat in those chairs and that people would have a renewed hunger for the Presence of God. I changed the lighting in the sanctuary to more of an intimate setting, bringing the lights down in the house and bringing the lights up on the cross that was located on the stage, highlighting it with red and white light. That was where the focus was to be; on what Jesus did on the cross for all of us. Throughout the day and into the night, people would come and sit in the presence of the Lord. I could hear crying and weeping as some people made it out of their chairs and down to the altar. A few people would climb the stairs of the stage and lay on their face at the feet of the cross. I never left my DJ booth area. I just let the people pray and work out what was going on between them and the Lord. I slept in my sleeping bag every night at the entrance to the sanctuary.

49

ONE AT A TIME

~

On day ten the Lord said, "You are not to read a newspaper or watch any form of TV until I say so." I thought, "Lord, I love to know what is going on locally, nationally and around the world." The Lord said, "No! I want you to put anointing oil on the door frame of the two doors that lead into the sanctuary and put a line of anointing oil on the carpet from one side of the door frame to the other." Then the Lord said, "I want you to anoint every chair in the sanctuary, every day, until I tell you to stop." I was able to get some anointing oil and did what the Lord asked me to do. I didn't tell anyone; I just did what I was told. On Sunday, day eleven at Emmanuel Fellowship, I met many more people from the congregation as they welcomed me. Pastor Frank told everyone I would be there for a few more weeks and that the church was open 24/7 for anyone who would like to come in to worship and pray. I was thinking, "Ok, Lord, now we're getting somewhere. You brought me to this house through all that I have been through. I'm sure this sanctuary will be full of people soon." The next few days a few more people came into the sanctuary. There were never more than a handful of people at one time, from early morning until late at night. Rachel, the church secretary, and a few others had become regulars, coming by everyday. Rachel had given me some music to listen to and a few others also shared music with me. I thanked them and told them that I would listen to the music when the Lord allowed me to. I was still rotating the same three CDs that I had been playing for two weeks.

The Lord was now stirring something deep inside of me. He had me start listening to the music I had collected over the years along with the new music I had just received. It was Wednesday, April 25th, and day fourteen of what had now become twenty-eight total days that the Lord was asking me to play music at Emmanuel Fellowship. People arrived for service that night and I continued to play music until the service began and started again when it ended. I would turn the music back on and it would run on repeat until I changed the CD. After everyone went home, I sat in the sanctuary and prayed, "Lord, I know You are among Your people and You visit them in their time of worship, but what will it take for you to dwell in this house, Lord? Send Your angels and prepare this house to be a dwelling place, not just a place for You to visit. Lord, send Your ministering angels to Your people in this church and throughout the Verde Valley."

Everyday the presence of the Lord grew stronger and stronger. It was Thursday morning, the 26th of April, when one of the morning worshippers came up to me and said, "Bobby, did you see the lady that was sitting in the seats over there?" She pointed in the direction of where I had seen one of the senior ladies sitting. I said, "Yes. She has been coming in the mornings for the past two weeks." The woman proceeded to tell me, "She just came up to me and gave me some money and asked me if I would buy you dinner." I asked, "Why don't we buy pizza for anyone who is around tonight?" She said that was a great idea. Then I asked her, "Did that woman say why she wanted to buy me dinner?" The lady replied, "She said that she has been coming here over the past few weeks and that, as she has been sitting in the presence of God with the worship music playing, she has been experiencing emotional healing and healing for issues that she had as a child. She said that she has gone to counseling and has gotten prayer for healing for over thirty-five years, but has not experienced anything like what has happened to her the past few weeks as she has come to worship and sit in the presence of the Lord. She said that she wanted to thank you for your obedience to the Lord; for being here night and day for the past few weeks." I replied that I was just trying to hang on to what the Lord has asked me to do at Emmanuel Fellowship. She smiled at me and said, "Thank you for what you are doing. We are praying for you and your family." I told her, "Thank you."

As she walked away, I couldn't help but think, "Lord, if it's Your will to bring people one at a time to be healed, give me the patience and the strength to endure." This was a totally different type of test from the Lord. It would be easy to be playing and ministering to a large crowd, but one at a time, 24/7, never knowing if I would see one person a day or ten, was a much tougher assignment. Then the Lord reminded me, "Are you here for them or for Me?" I said, "I am here for You, Lord. As I worship You and seek Your face, it is You that brings healing and deliverance to Your people." The next few days, the Lord was speaking to me about recording worship CDs in the sanctuary. I had been playing CDs that I had previously recorded and now I was going to start recording new worship CDs as the Lord led me. That was exciting for me and it was something that was ready to creatively come out of me. The Lord gave me the titles of the first four CDs I was to record in the sanctuary. They were: "Set Me Free," "Enter In," "Behind the Veil," and "The Throne Room."

50

THANK YOU FOR BEING OBEDIENT

~

What started off as seven days of 24-hour worship at Emmanuel Fellowship turned into twenty-eight days, then forty days, and then the Lord told me I would be there for six months. So, for six months I lived in the church and kept the doors open 24/7 with the help of Pastor Frank and a few others. After six months, or two hundred three days, of no television, no radio, and no newspapers, I was able to go back to Phoenix with my family. However, even then, I was still going back and forth from Phoenix to Cottonwood. All three of my children made a trip or two with me to Emmanuel Fellowship to meet the people, the Pastor and staff of this church, and some of the people from other churches that visited Emmanuel Fellowship on a regular basis.

After six months at Emmanuel, I didn't pull the music out of the church. Pastor Frank and his staff had the music playing 24/7 even if the doors were not open 24/7. I left a complete sound system, which I gave to the church, in the sanctuary so that the music could continue. Over the past year, a few people have come from Cottonwood to meet my wife. I can't tell you how much I have felt loved and accepted by Pastor Frank and the congregation of Emmanuel Fellowship. They have been so supportive of my family and me. I will never forget the time that some of the prayer warriors from another church were visiting Emmanuel. They were from a town nearby and heard that the church was open 24/7. There were six women that came one morning to worship. They were at the altar crying when one of them came up to me and said, "Do you know the warfare that surrounds you and your family?" I answered, "Yes, I do." She said, "We have been praying and waiting for this for years and when we heard what the Lord was doing here, we had to come." She was crying as she spoke to me. She said, "We will pray for you and your family." She started walking back to the altar when she stopped and turned back to me and said, "Bobby, thank you for being obedient to the Lord." I just smiled and thought, "If she only knew what it took to get here and how much it has taken for me to stay here hour after hour, day after day." But it was all about simply being obedient to the Lord.

51

WHAT IS TRUE WORSHIP

~

Today in the American church, I am in shock at the way we worship when we come into the House of God. I guess it's just me but I can't figure out how we are supposed to come into the presence of God and invite Him into our time of worship with four or five songs followed by the Word or sermon or a commentary on life shared with the congregation. We were created to worship the Lord. Most of us, as we enter the time of worship in our church, are still trying to shake off the cares and trials of life that overwhelm us and our families. Then, just when we are about to enter into the presence of the Lord, it is time to sit down for announcements, the offering, and maybe a message from the media department about upcoming events and programs at the church. So many people need to be set free, healed and delivered; and that's just those who already know Jesus Christ as Lord and Savior. What about those who do not know Him and need to? I'm afraid we have boxed the Holy Spirit and kept Him from having the freedom to move among God's people as we gather together. Our programs are so time sensitive that it drives me crazy. Maybe we should have people at the front door of the church with buckets. We could drop our watches into the buckets as we enter the church and grab a watch out of the bucket when we leave. It would keep the pastors and the congregation from checking the time every ten minutes. Then maybe the Lord would have the freedom to move in our services. You might think I'm joking, but I'm not.

I have always enjoyed talking to the older saints in the body of

Christ. I love the wisdom and life experiences they have to share if only we would take the time to talk with them. I have had many discussions over the years about what it was like for them "back in the day" when they were young, when they were raising up their families, when it came to church and worship times, and when many of them experienced the moving of the Holy Spirit in their lives. These are people in their seventies and older. I ask them, "Back in the day, when the Holy Spirit moved on the service, didn't you stay at the altar until you and the Lord were done, even if that was all afternoon and into the night, depending on the denomination and the type of church?" Many of them shared that that was indeed the way they had grown up and that the church doors were always open, 24/7, for anyone to come into the church to pray.

So, apparently that was what the Lord had asked me to do at Emmanuel Fellowship, to be a gate keeper to keep the House of God open and the fire lit around the clock. Over the years, I have never recorded any worship CD unless I felt a really strong leading from the Lord. I needed the Lord to anoint what I was doing. Sure, just putting some music together would be uplifting and could minister to people, but I needed it to be so much more. It's the anointing that breaks the chains, sets people free and opens up the hardest of hearts to receive healing. I know people are drawn to those with a strong anointing in whatever gift they move in for the Lord, and that is okay. It is a problem when we become enamored with the gift, and those with it, instead of with the Giver of the gift. Everyone that I have met or studied who has had a strong anointing has paid a heavy price for the anointing that they walk in, none more than Christ. You know what I am talking about. The trials, tribulations and brokenness of their lives allowed many to be used greatly for the Lord. I have always known it is not me and my talent or gifts that touch people and bring healing; it is the Lord Jesus Christ and the Power of the Holy Spirit. I'm sorry if I have spent a few minutes on this subject, but it is the most important thing I would like to share about the way I worship, why I worship, and the drive behind the worship that I have produced for the Lord.

I played music in nightclubs for over fourteen years and I'm sure that I entertained them and I know I was not leading them closer to the things of God, but in the opposite direction. It is an honor and amazing that the Creator of the Universe would use me and allow me to create worship CDs that would bring healing and deliverance to people. I have always said to those people who see me playing live that it is an honor to play for the King. Over the years I have found that I can't make people hungry for God, or make them worship God, but I can create an atmosphere of hungry worship through my own life and my obedience to His call on my life and my family. It is not an encounter with me that can change anyone's life, but an encounter with Jesus Christ that will change someone's life, like it did mine. My prayer is that, hopefully, the Christ in me will draw people to desire to know Him. This is why the worship music, the lights and the atmosphere that I create for the Lord are serious things to me. If Jesus' name is lifted up, He will draw all men unto Himself (John 12:32). I personally have seen it and experienced it a thousand times over. It is not about playing a song on your CD player. It is about saturating your home, your car and your life with worship. I have told people over and over to fill their lives with worship for the King and with His Word. I have talked to so many people who have taken the CDs that I have made and played them 24/7 in their homes, cars, office, and as the name of Jesus has been lifted up, the anointing of God has touched them. These people have shared some amazing stories of healing and intimate times of worship with the Lord. To God Be All the Glory! Worship isn't Sunday and Wednesday at church. It is a lifestyle. And as we create a place for the Lord, not to visit but to dwell, we will experience times with the Lord that we didn't even know were possible.

There are so many stories to tell about this part of my journey at Emmanuel. It has been a year and a half and the worship continues to play. I thought, "How can I possibly share all of the stories from amazing visitations from angels to drug addicts that came to sleep at the door of the church and later slept in the church and were set free and so much more?" After much prayer, I have decided to write about and interview these people so you can hear for yourself of the many miracles.

That however will be another book...